W. H. Bennett

The Mishna

As illustrating the Gospels

W. H. Bennett

The Mishna
As illustrating the Gospels

ISBN/EAN: 9783743355293

Manufactured in Europe, USA, Canada, Australia, Japa

Cover: Foto ©Lupo / pixelio.de

Manufactured and distributed by brebook publishing software (www.brebook.com)

W. H. Bennett

The Mishna

THE MISHNA

Cambridge:
PRINTED BY C. J. CLAY, M.A. AND SON,
AT THE UNIVERSITY PRESS.

THE MISHNA

AS ILLUSTRATING

THE GOSPELS

BY

W. H. BENNETT B.A.

(M.A. LONDON)
FRY HEBREW SCHOLAR OF ST JOHN'S COLLEGE CAMBRIDGE
TYRWHITT SCHOLAR

Published in accordance with the requirements of Mrs Ann Fry's Hebrew Scholarship

---

CAMBRIDGE
DEIGHTON BELL AND CO.
LONDON GEORGE BELL AND SONS
1884

PREFACE.

IN the following essay an attempt has been made to arrange and in a slight measure to interpret some of the facts as to the Mishna and the Gospels in relation to one another. The lessons to be drawn from the errors of the Pharisees are in general so much better known than the facts about these errors, that it has not been felt necessary to insist much upon these lessons and I have tried, probably with only very moderate success, to deal with the Mishna in some spirit of sympathy. For only thus is it possible to deal fairly with any teachers and the record of their teaching.

The extracts from the Mishna are taken from the translations of Rabbis de Sola and Raphall and of Barclay, from Dr Taylor's '*Sayings of the Jewish Fathers*' and from the Latin translation of Surenhusius.

The historical data are mainly derived from Milman's *History of the Jews*, Jost's *Geschichte der Israeliten*, and the article by Dr Schiller-Szinessy on the *Mishna* in the *Encyclopaedia Britannica*.

For the suggestion of a subject and for criticism on parts of the essay I am indebted to Rev. R. Sinker, M.A., B.D., of Trinity College.

CONTENTS.

CHAP.		PAGE
I.	The Mishna	1
II.	The Mishna and the Gospels as based on Oral Tradition	13
III.	The Mishna as illustrating the Gospels generally	20
IV.	The Pharisees	29
V.	The Sabbath	53
VI.	The Status of Women	67
VII.	Ethics and Doctrine	79
VIII.	Vows. The Poor	92
IX.	Relation of the Mishna and the Gospels to the Old Testament	98
X.	Subsequent History of the Mishna and the Gospels	107
	Appendix	114

CHAPTER I.

THE MISHNA.

THE Mishna is an authoritative application of Mosaic law to later times, a Jewish law-book of the third century, A.D. As the ancient laws of the Pentateuch claim divine authority and form the essential part of the Jewish religious writings, so do the laws of the Mishna claim the authority of Divine revelation given to Moses and handed down by oral tradition. It is also one of the earliest extant Hebrew books after the close of the Old Testament Canon, thus continuing after an interval of centuries the line of Hebrew Literature. It links the Judaism of the Old Testament, of the Maccabees, of the Herods, with that persistent unalterable Judaism which has endured down to our own times. It professes to record laws and customs which must have regulated the lives of orthodox Jews during the ministry of Christ and the spread of Christianity.

<small>General statement.</small>

On the one hand, these laws and customs grew up between the close of the Old Testament Canon and the compilation of the Mishna and so represent Jewish life and its tendencies during that period; and on the other, these laws and customs as set forth by the Mishna and interpreted in its commentaries have done much to determine Jewish life ever since.

The estimation in which the Mishna was once held by almost all Jews and is still held by many, may be illustrated from an official translation of certain of its treatises. Writing[1] in 1842, and speaking of one class amongst their fellow Israelites, the translators say in their preface:

"There can be no doubt that to the Israelite, who believes in the divinity of an oral law—who thinks the salvation of his soul depends on such belief—but to whom the Mishna in the Hebrew is a sealed book—there can be no doubt that to such a man, if he be *rational* as well as pious, the present translation must be highly acceptable, as mere belief in the contents of a book not understood can confer no claim to heavenly reward".

The Mishna is 'the fundamental document of the oral law of the Jews[2]'.

According to Jost[3] the Mishna was to be to the Jews 'a new Fatherland' to compensate them for their losses. From it the life of later Rabbinic Judaism drew its nourishment and strength, and to the Mishna this later Judaism devoted its literary industry.

The Gemara says that he who reads Scripture without learning Mishna is a boor [4,5].

---

[1] Eighteen Treatises from the Mishna, translated by Rev. D. A. de Sola and the Rev. M. J. Raphall.
[2] Art. Mishna, *Encycl. Brit.* Dr Schiller-Szinessy.
[3] Jost, *Gesch. Isrl.* Bk. XIII. Ch. I.
[4] Wagenseil, *Sota*, p. 516.
[5] Rabbinowicz, in the preface to his *Législation Criminelle du Talmud* tells us how, inspired by his zeal for the Talmud, he worked all day and all the evening in a *café*, because he could not afford to pay for a fire, and dined for 13 or 11 sous a day.

THE MISHNA.

A leading part in the compilation of the Mishna is always assigned to Rabbi Judah Hakkadosh (the Holy), who flourished about the end of the second century. Jost speaks of him as producing the first written edition of the Mishna, the present form of the work being a later recension. Dr Schiller-Szinessy and other authorities maintain that Rabbi Judah only collected and supplemented and arranged the oral tradition, and did not commit it to writing. But he says that the Mishna belongs to Rabbi Judah 'in great measure and in more than one sense[1]'.

In addition to his name of 'the Holy', he was called Han-Nasi (the Prince) as president of the Sanhedrim and head of the Jews of Tiberias. On account of his distinguished position, he is frequently spoken of simply as 'Rabbi'. He inherited his position from his father; and in earlier times his ancestors Gamaliel, the teacher of St Paul, and the celebrated Hillel had been presidents of the Jewish school of traditional law. In the days of Rabbi Judah the Sanhedrim was mainly occupied in discussing the application of the law of Moses. It is doubtful whether cases were submitted to them that they might judge actual criminals or decide matters in dispute between man and man. But they were much occupied with abstract points and imaginary cases. While individual Rabbis had their schools and discussed these matters with their pupils, the Rabbis themselves met for similar discussion in the Sanhedrim under the presidency of Judah Han-Nasi. He too had his own private school, whither resorted Jewish scholars from far and near. In earlier life he himself was such a scholar frequenting the schools and hearing the sayings of the older Rabbis,

[1] Art. Mishna, *Encycl. Brit.*

and now, after the usual custom of Jewish teachers, he handed on these sayings to his scholars with additions and interpretations of his own.

The Mishna is the written record of such sayings, but as we have already said it is matter of controversy when and by whom an edition of the Mishna was committed to writing. Jost[1] says it is probable that Rabbi Judah wrote a book as a private work, but that officially the Mishna would still be transmitted orally and that the date of any official written book would be much later. Dr Schiller-Szinessy[2] emphatically denies that the Mishna could have been written down for centuries after the time of Rabbi Judah, though he admits that there were small collections of notes kept in secret. Would it be permissible to suppose that Rabbi Judah might at least have collections of notes more copious than those of any other students of Mishna? If we have to admit that the codification of the oral tradition was accomplished and transmitted purely by memory, we, in these days of note books and printing-presses can only regard Rabbi Judah and his successors with the greater admiration[3].

Not only was he qualified for his arduous task by hereditary aptitude and acquired learning, but he was wealthy and is said to have been intimate with Romans of high position, notably with an emperor called 'Antoninus[4]'.

His life was spent chiefly at Beth-Shearim[5] and Sepphoris.

[1] Jost, Bk. XIII. Note 25.
[2] Art. Mishna, *Encycl. Brit.*
[3] It is indeed said in Yoma III. 1 that Queen He'ena of Adiabene, a contemporary of Christ, had the section Sota written on a tablet of gold; but even if this is true, it would scarcely apply to the whole section.
[4] This 'Antoninus' has been identified with Marcus Aurelius, Caracalla and other Roman emperors. Many writers refuse to believe the story.
[5] N.E. of Sepphoris. Graetz, *Gesch. der Juden*, IV. 234.

As to his personal character little is known; the failing of his family was pride, and he himself is said not to have been altogether free from it[1].

When the Mishna was compiled the hopes of the Jews had been twice raised to the highest pitch only to be utterly disappointed. For the Jewish wars of 70, when the temple was destroyed, and of 132 (the revolt of Barchochabh) had both been fought with partial success at first and then there came in each case defeat, massacre and wholesale slavery. In the Christian Church at this time the great teachers of Alexandria and Carthage were developing doctrine and maintaining the enthusiasm of their followers. *Circumstances.*

The Roman Empire had seen or saw in the near distance the tokens of the close of the prosperous era of the Antonines, and was experiencing or was soon to experience the vicissitudes of military anarchy, tempered now and then by able military despots. Possibly a sense of insecurity, caused partly by the disastrous results of the Jewish wars and partly by the unsettled state of the Empire, may have had to do with the committing to writing of the Jewish tradition[2]. At the conclusion of each revolt the Rabbis had been scattered, and after that of Barchochabh an attempt seems to have been made to put an end to the succession. The substitution of a written manuscript for oral tradition might be a safeguard against similar attempts.

Or even if the Mishna were not then committed to writing, much might be gained by collecting scattered and often fading traditions and arranging them so that the

---

[1] Yet he is spoken of as the 'humble', Horaioth f. 14 in Jost, XIII. 10.
[2] See above, similar causes would act still more powerfully later on.

memory might more easily retain the whole[1]. As yet there was still a large Jewish community in Galilee and the Romans tolerated the Jewish schools, but there was no guarantee that this state of things would continue.

Then, too, this is the age of Papinian and other great Roman jurists, and possibly the enthusiasm for codifying laws was infectious[2].

Antiquity claimed for laws. What then was the antiquity of the laws codified? They claim in part to be an unwritten tradition handed down from Moses, and in part to be the sayings of various Rabbis through whom the tradition was handed down.

The succession is given thus at the beginning of the Pirke Aboth:

"Moses received the law from Sinai and delivered it to Joshua, and Joshua to the elders, and the elders to the prophets, and the prophets to the men of the great Synagogue", then "Simon the Just", "Antigonus of Socho", "Joseph ben Joezer of Tseredah and Joseph ben Jochanan of Jerusalem", "Joshua ben Perachiah and Matthai the Arbelite", "Judah ben Tabbai and Simon ben Shatach", "Shemaiah and Abtalion", "Hillel and Shammai", "Johanan ben Zakkai". The usual formula is 'so and so received of so and so', and occurs last in the instance, "Johanan ben Zakkai received of Hillel". The Mishna also quotes many other sages, notably the Gamaliel of Acts and his descendants down to Rabbi Judah himself.

The Mishna is divided into six[3] books and 63 treatises,

---

[1] Cf. Art. Mishna, *Encycl. Brit.*
[2] Cf. Milman's *Hist. of Jews*, II. 478.
[3] The number of treatises as given by different authorities varies from 60 to 63.

the division being according to the main body of the subject-matter, digressions being freely allowed.

Its contents may be variously classified, for instance, we may adopt a threefold division: Character of contents.

(*a*) The traditional rules or Mishna proper, which are simply stated.

(*b*) Opinions and decisions of Rabbis, individually or collectively (as 'the Sages'), with which may be classed various moral and religious sayings.

(*c*) Leading cases or precedents, together with other illustrative stories and with matters of antiquarian or general interest.

It would be easy to subdivide these classes and yet fail to embrace all the contents of the Mishna. Surely no other law book was ever so given to irrelevant gossip. And yet there is sufficient 'system to prevent the confusion from being artistic', and far too much 'confusion to allow the system to be scientific'.

There is indeed a general method underlying very many of the treatises, and up to a certain point such a treatise may be developed from its fundamental maxim almost as if by mathematical formula: thus: The Pentateuch lays down a [1]general rule, 'Thou shalt not sow thy field with a mingled seed'.

The question arises[2] 'What are "mingled seed"?' and the investigation is pursued with laborious patience through all the varieties of grain and vegetables. 'Barley and oats

---

[1] N. B. The general rule is not quoted, but it is assumed that the reader is familiar with it.
[2] Kilaim 1.

are not mingled seed, nor spelt and rye &c., &c.' for several paragraphs, with occasional notes that 'cucumbers and melons are not mingled seed, but Rabbi Judah says they are'.

[1] Later on the question arises as to the space to be left between vines and sown land. Rabbi Judah tells a little anecdote of a man at Zalmon, who worked his vineyard and sown land in a complicated and doubtful manner. When, however, the matter was brought before the sages, they acquitted him of any breach of the law against sowing mingled seed.

Much of what at first sight appears to be antiquarian really falls under this formula. For instance the treatises 'Measures' (of the temple), 'The Day' (of Atonement), 'The Perpetual' (or daily sacrifice) are really laws intended for the restored temple.

Then there are anecdotes seemingly having only a mnemonic connection with the context; anecdotes suggested to the writer by the subject he was dealing with, and considered too good to be lost.

Thus in discussing the desecration of idols[2] the following occurs[3]:

"The elders were asked in Rome, 'If God has no pleasure in idolatry, why does He not destroy it'? They replied to the Romans, 'If the idolaters were serving a thing not necessary to the world, He would destroy it, but they serve the sun, moon and stars and the signs of the zodiac. Shall He destroy His world on account of the fools'?"

[1] Kilaim IV. 9.
[2] With a view to their use.
[3] Abodah Zarah, IV. 7.

The moral and religious sayings are chiefly collected in the Pirke Aboth.

More will have to be said as to this want of regularity in comparing the arrangement of the Mishna with that of the Gospels. We may however again quote from de Sola and Raphall. In a note at the beginning of the treatise Demai they say: 'It must be remarked that the Mishna nowhere confines itself to the subject only of which it professes to treat; but that remarks and opinions are occasionally introduced bearing no reference to the subject which precedes or succeeds them'.

We might notice briefly the relation of the Mishna to the Gemara. The Gemara is a kind of commentary on the Mishna, and the Mishna and Gemara together make up the Talmud[1]. The Gemara explains the Mishna, investigates its sources and also supplements it. Besides this it abounds in irrelevant digressions and anecdotes. Perhaps one might say very roughly that the Gemara is to the Mishna as the Mishna is to the Pentateuch. There are two Gemaras, the Jerusalem compiled in the fourth century and the Babylonian in the fifth. <small>Relation to the Gemara.</small>

Dr Schiller-Szinessy says: 'The language of the Mishna, although pure and indeed purer than the language of several books of the Bible, was so concise and terse that it could not be understood without a commentary'. <small>Obscure style.</small>

This elliptical style may perhaps be compared to that of a telegram which has to be expanded before it can be under- <small>Elliptical.</small>

---

[1] While it is true that in the present arrangement of the Talmud the commentary on the Mishna is called Gemara, it appears that Gemara was originally a general term for Rabbinical learning. Cf. Taylor, *Sayings of Jewish Fathers*, p. 112.

stood. For instance in the following quotation the words in brackets are part of the expansion and have no counterpart in the Hebrew. "[Damages awarded to her in compensation for] insult or injury belong to her. Rabbi Judah ben Bethera saith: [if the injury inflicted on her is] hidden, two-thirds [of the damages recovered] belong to her and one-third to him [the husband][1]".

Without the words in brackets it would read thus, "insult or injury belong to her. Rabbi Judah ben Bethera saith hidden two-thirds belong to her, and one-third to him". Surely this would be sufficiently unintelligible to the ordinary reader.

Enigmatical.

In parts the language of the Mishna is highly figurative and enigmatical: for instance, 'Be a tail to lions and not a head to foxes'[2]. 'Warm thyself before the fire of the wise but beware of their embers'[3].

Sometimes instead of these brief enigmatical sentences there are parables almost equally obscure and contrasting somewhat with the simplicity of most of the Gospel parables.

Range of subjects.

The subjects with which the Mishna deals range from minute points of etiquette such as the proper place to put one's napkin after dinner; to the most profound questions of theology. It treats of civil and criminal, ceremonial and moral law; aiming in fact at being an exhaustive treatise on every detail of the whole duty of man. It deals however almost entirely with the outward observances and has little to say about the inner life.

Naturally the treatment of these outward observances is

[1] Ketuboth, VI. 1, de Sola and Raphall.
[2] Pirke Aboth, IV. 22.
[3] Pirke Aboth, II. 14.

often tedious and dwells with tiresome minuteness on trivial details. The reader gets impatient and almost indignant as one great rabbi after another delivers his opinion as to the arrangement of vegetables and fruit-trees in the fields, or the question whether a man may go out with a wooden leg on the Sabbath.

But it seems that even to a Jew of the present day all this is quite natural, and perhaps we cannot better close this general view of the character of the Mishna than by illustrating its spirit by the following quotations from a recent Jewish writer. *Spirit of Mishna.*

'The duty of wearing Phylacteries, which is so rigorously enjoined, that he who dispenses with them is considered altogether impious, is so vaguely indicated in the Law that without tradition we should not know their form'.

'We often read in the Pentateuch that he who works on the Sabbath shall be put to death, and the Scripture nowhere defines what work is or what kind of work is forbidden'.

'With tradition all these difficulties are removed, it supplies the silence of the text, explains apparent contradictions and pleonasms, gives to the words of the Scripture their true meaning, and to laws the development necessary for their application'.

'The sacrifice of Elijah on Carmel was a contravention of the law. Deut. xii. 13'.

'There must therefore have been a tradition which in such cases authorises these contraventions'.

'The Pentateuch seems to be silent on the most fundamental and most consoling truths, such as the immortality of the soul...God has transmitted them verbally, with the means of finding them in the text'.

'A complementary tradition was necessary and indispensable'[1].

[1] Klein, *La Vérité sur le Talmud*, pp. 12—15.

CHAPTER II.

The Mishna and the Gospels as based on Oral Tradition.

WHAT has already been said of the Mishna, as the result of oral tradition, suggests one broad ground of comparison with the Gospels. *Origin of the Gospels.*

According to the most probable view[1] of the origin of the Synoptic Gospels, they too are the result of oral tradition. Indeed according to any view they must be so to some extent, but the view in question lays special stress on this feature. It is supposed that the written Gospels were derived directly from the preaching of the Apostles. The substance of this preaching was the history and sayings of Christ. In time the contents of their message shaped themselves by a kind of natural selection, certain of the sayings, certain portions of the history appealed more readily and with more effect to the Apostles' audience. Then when the demand arose for a written Gospel, this Gospel would be simply the record of the preaching of the Apostles, in the form determined by much experience among many peoples.

[1] Westcott, *Introduction to the Gospels*, ch. III.

14 THE MISHNA AND THE GOSPELS

Oral sources.

Without entering into the controversies as to the authorship of the Gospels and while accepting the ordinary views it is easy to point out the oral nature of their sources. As far as we know Christ wrote nothing, His disciples committed none of His sayings to writing during His life. His teaching consisted of spoken sayings doubtless often repeated, and fixing themselves in the memory partly by the force of Christ's enthusiasm and the commanding influence of His character, partly by the striking nature of the sayings themselves, partly doubtless by frequent repetition.

In some such way would S. Matthew come to remember the sayings of the Sermon on the Mount and at last after years of preaching commit them to writing in their present form.

In the case of S. Mark the tradition would not be so immediate, we have no reason to believe that he was a constant hearer of Christ. Early Christian writers speak of him as recording the substance of S. Peter's preaching. So that here S. Peter hears from Christ and S. Mark from S. Peter. S. Luke again is said to have followed in his Gospel the preaching of S. Paul. At any rate he professes to be indebted in his narrative to 'eyewitnesses and ministers of the word'. If he derived anything from S. Paul, e.g. the account of the Last Supper, it would imply at least two links in the chain of tradition between S. Luke and Christ. S. Paul himself must have been indebted to some eyewitness, directly or indirectly, for his account.

It will be obvious that the essential fact of oral tradition is not affected, if we refuse to accept the statements as to the dependence of S. Mark and S. Luke on S. Peter and S. Paul. For these evangelists, not being themselves eyewitnesses, would depend on what they heard from those whose connection with Christ was closer and more constant. Another reference to the handing down of truth by word of mouth occurs in Hebr. ii. 3, where the writer speaks of the confirmation of the promise of salvation to his readers and himself by those that heard Christ. Moreover the early Christian writers appeal rather to a still living tradition than to written Gospels[1].

This method of preserving and communicating truth was exactly that of the Jewish Schools, and the committing to writing of the Gospels under the pressure of possible lapse of tradition is very similar to the committing to writing of the Jewish tradition in the Mishna. One difference is that the Christians broke loose from the prejudice against a written Gospel much sooner than the Jews and anticipated them by more than a century, or perhaps by several centuries. *Oral tradition in the Jewish Schools.*

In the Mishna we have the sayings of the editor himself, just as in the Gospels we have the comments of their authors. We have the sayings of Simon, son of Gamaliel, whom Judah himself had heard, as S. Matthew and S. John had heard Christ. We have traditions at third and fourth hand as in S. Mark and S. Luke, and then the tradition stretches away into the more remote past. There are also in the Mishna as we have it sayings added by teachers who succeeded Rabbi Judah. It is as if some one had gathered up the floating traditions of the second century, some few possibly authentic fragments of which still survive, and had incorporated these floating traditions in a new edition of the Gospels. Nor are there wanting critics who would have us believe that our *Various forms of tradition in the Mishna.*

---

[1] Westcott, *Introduction to the Gospels*, ch. III.

present Gospels are a comparatively late recension of that Gospel, which formed the substance of the Apostles' preaching. In fact there is a controversy as to how soon the Gospel was committed to writing, just as there is a controversy as to how soon the Mishna was committed to writing. The arguments by which Jewish writers maintain that the Mishna, if only committed to writing at a late date, faithfully reproduces the earlier traditions; these arguments will also tend to prove that, even if the Gospel was transmitted for a century by oral tradition, it yet faithfully reproduces the earlier preaching.

Authority of tradition.

The unhesitating acceptance of the record of tradition by the Jews in the case of the Mishna helps us to see that all who shared their habits and training would be prepared to accord a similar recognition to the record of Christian tradition in the Gospels. When a new work appears now-a-days we ask on what evidence of documents or monuments or coins the book is based: the Jew asked from whom the speaker or author had heard what he asserted or recorded. If the answer was 'Rabbi Gamaliel' or 'Rabbi Akiba' he was satisfied, and doubtless equally so if it was Rabbi Dosithai in the name of Rabbi Meir or Rabbi Simeon ben Judah in the name of Rabbi Simeon ben Jochai. So the Christian Jew might ask concerning the account of the Magi 'Who taught this'? The answer would be 'the Holy Apostle Matthew': or again he might ask as to the parable of the seed growing secretly and the answer would be 'the Evangelist Mark in the name of the Holy Apostle Peter'. To the Jew such answers would be natural and satisfactory.

Tendencies of tradition as

Then too the principles which determine the contents of the Mishna and of the Gospels are in part the same. In each case the vitality of the tradition was tested by years, in some cases by generations, of teaching. The ultimate record only contained that which survived the test. Of course the main tendency would be to neglect and forget that which did not prove itself practically useful; and yet in many cases sayings and stories will be remembered and recorded for no apparent reason but simply because of some special working of the laws of association in the minds of those who handed on the tradition. It will be plain that the working of these common tendencies will still leave wide room for differences in the character of the contents of the Mishna and the Gospels, and indeed there are enormous differences. The causes to which these differences are due will be obvious to anyone.

But to return to the influence of the process of tradition on the contents of the Mishna and the Gospels; to us it may seem that minor truths and transient interests occupy too large a space, some things may seem irrelevant and some unintelligible. Much that we expect to find is absent. We should not willingly lose a word that throws light in any way on the life and teaching of Christ, and yet some might think that less might have been said of the traditions of the Pharisees and more of the great evangelical doctrine of justification by faith or that the principle of apostolic succession might have been set forth more clearly. We may wonder at what seems to us the involved vagueness of the prophecy of 'the last things'; we may not understand how an obscure incident like that of the 'young man[1]' with 'a linen cloth cast about him' is relevant to the general narrative.

If we turn to the Mishna we shall find that the same

[1] Mark xiv. 51, 52.

process of natural selection by oral tradition has destroyed in a much greater degree the symmetry and coherence of the record. There it seems as if the popular taste and the atmosphere of the schools had chosen to have hardly anything but minor truths and transient interests; the traditions of the Pharisees drive the great truths of morality and religion into odd corners. It is difficult to point out special examples of irrelevancy in the Mishna, because after reading a few sections the student gets a general idea that everything is relevant to everything else, and it seems almost natural to discuss in a treatise on the new year the reason why we are not told the names of the elders who ascended Sinai with Moses[1]. The reason is that the Mishna wanders on like a man thinking aloud in a desultory fashion and gives the chance links in the train of thought, while the Gospel constantly omits them.

Influence of oral tradition on arrangement.
The same facts help us to understand the difficulty in either case of finding a scientific or chronological arrangement. Events and sayings were remembered and finally recorded as they were associated together and suggested each other in the minds of those who remembered them. They might be associated because of their connection in time or because they were similar in subject, but men's reminiscences are grouped according to many less obvious laws than those of connection in time or similarity in subject.

In the Mishna a long discussion about the payment of tithes for land in Ammon and Moab interrupts the rules for purifying the hands; and again the account of the signs of

[1] Rosh Hashanah II. 9. Exod. xxiv. 2.

the coming of the Messiah occurs in the treatise on the 'Waters of Jealousy'.

Similarly in the Gospels the arrangement does not always admit of easy explanation, and different Evangelists connect the same sayings with very different contexts.

Again, in the Gospels, much is common to the three Synoptic Gospels and is called by many the Triple Tradition. Yet there is much not contained in this Triple Tradition, but preserved by one or two Evangelists. In a somewhat similar manner the Mishna may be supposed to represent the main stream of Jewish tradition. But there are other works, the 'Tosifta' and 'Bereitha', for which some claim an equal antiquity and to which the Jews accord a modified authority, and these preserve supplementary traditions. *Supplementary traditions.*

Also it may be noticed that, while separate Gospels seem to present discrepancies, the Mishna does not hesitate to record the varying decisions or reminiscences of different authorities. For instance the Rabbis disagree as to whether Ecclesiastes and Canticles render the hands unclean, i.e. are canonical books[1]. *Discrepancies in tradition.*

[1] Yadaim IV. 5.

CHAPTER III.

THE MISHNA AS ILLUSTRATING THE GOSPELS GENERALLY.

So far the grounds of comparison may be considered certain, both Mishna and Gospel are due to tradition. The traditional character of the Mishna is universally acknowledged and is proved by both internal and external evidence. In the case of the Gospels there is at any rate a strong element of tradition.

Illustration in subject-matter.

But we wish to use the Mishna to illustrate not only the method of composition of the Gospels but also their subject matter. Before we can do so it is necessary to enquire how far the customs, feelings and doctrine of the Jews as given in the Mishna are similar to those of the Jews in the time of Christ.

Interval between Gospels and Mishna.

On the one hand we have to remember that a period of from 150 to 200 years had elapsed between the death of Christ and the publication of the Mishna, and that during this period the Jews had been crushed by two disastrous wars; their capital and its temple had been destroyed; and Jerusalem had been replaced by a new city Œlia Capitolina, from which the Jews were excluded.

Effects of the interval.

At first sight a period so long and eventful might be expected to work much change in the customs of social and

religious life. If we look back 150 years to the reign of
George II., or 200 years to that of Charles II., and remember
the wars and constitutional changes of the period, the pro-
gress in science, the railways, telegraph and penny post, we
might be tempted to say that a student would find little in
English life and literature of to-day to illustrate English
life of 150 or 200 years ago. But a moment's thought shows
us how much still remains the same. For instance the
Prayer-Book is almost identically the same, and many of the
forms of social and commercial life, many of the ceremonies
of Parliament and the law courts are the same. Then too
the principles and position of the High Church party of to-
day illustrate those of the High Church party of the time of
Laud; and the spirit of 'No Popery' survives to help us to
understand the long maintenance of the penal laws against
the Catholics.

If all this is true in Western progressive England, how
much more so in the changeless East, in a nation that clung
tenaciously to the past, governed by scholars whose whole
theory of learning was to remember, to reproduce, to interpret what had been handed down, as they believed, even
from Moses. If to-day, after the lapse of eighteen centuries,
the dresses, customs and language of the East still afford
material for illustrating both Old and New Testament, how
much more a book compiled not later than the middle of the
third century after Christ and professing to contain traditions
of teachers from Ezra to its own time? Men in those days
did not ask continually: 'Who will shew us any new thing'?
New things meant revolutions or calamities[1], the new things,

[1] נוֹסָפֹת Is. xv. 9. 'Added things', i.e. according to some, 'new
evils'; cf. 'res novæ' for 'revolutions'.

the revolutions of the Jews had been disastrous, and they tried to maintain all that linked their life with older times. For these older times, especially when remembered after many years of misfortune, were more glorious or at any rate more peaceful.

The changes that have altered our life and language are not so much our wars and revolutions as the railways, the telegraph and the postal system, the increase of intercourse between men and nations, and the immediate knowledge of contemporaneous history all over the world far and near. It is true that the unity of the Roman Empire led to much intercommunication between its parts and that the Jews and the Roman officials were perhaps the greatest travellers of their day. It is true too that the Jews then as now corresponded with one another and knew each other's doings better than any other set of people. But at their best the opportunities for intercommunication afforded by the Roman Empire were far inferior to those of modern civilisation. Moreover the Jews lived in the world and were not of the world, and had no sympathy with heathen life and its customs. And the Rabbis consciously and strenuously resisted all influences from the Gentiles and doubtless even from the Jews of the Dispersion. The Dispersion was to humbly accept the law from them, they would not learn from the Dispersion. Now the Mishna belongs to the Judaism of the Rabbis.

The chain of Rabbinical succession seems to have been unbroken. The Sanhedrim is said to have left Jerusalem before the final siege and to have established itself at Jamnia. Nor did the Romans molest them till the revolt of Barchochabh. Even then the Rabbis in defiance of

THE GOSPELS GENERALLY. 23

Roman decrees appointed successors to their office and provided for the transmission of the tradition.

There is too a certain local continuity about the Judaism of the Mishna. The seat of the patriarchate at this time was Tiberias in Galilee, and before that had been Sepphoris in Galilee. Judah Hakkadosh spent the later years of his life at Sepphoris. Neither Tiberias nor Sepphoris suffered much in the first Jewish war. Sepphoris first obtained permission from Josephus to protect itself with walls and then submitted to Vespasian before he entered Palestine and received from him a Roman garrison. Tiberias was spared through the intercession of Agrippa[1].

The records of the war of Barchochabh are too scanty to enable us to say whether these cities suffered during his revolt. If they escaped a second time they were exceptionally fortunate. But at any rate we find Jewish communities at both Sepphoris and Tiberias soon after the revolt[2]. Thus the Mishna was compiled in a district where the practice of Jewish customs had gone on for centuries almost without interruption.

We have therefore to take into account the attachment of the Jews to their past, their trustful reverence for traditional teaching, the mutual hatred between Jew and Gentile and the consequent estrangement of the Jew from all sympathy of life and thought with the Gentile: we have to bear in mind the unbroken chain of Rabbinical succession and the comparative tranquillity of the seats of Rabbinical learning, whereby the Eastern tendency to the maintenance of old customs was allowed fair scope. Then, though in the

[1] *Vita Josephi*, § 65.
[2] Jost, Bk. XII. ch. 13.

most careful and laborious oral teaching there must be something lost in course of time, and though even in the conservative and stationary East, a school of learning can scarcely busy itself with one subject for generations without adding much by way of development or interpretation, yet we may conclude that in substance and spirit the position of the Jews in the Mishna is that of the Jews of the first century. Especially as the Mishna is essentially a law-book and law is conservative, and the forms and records of the law are a perfect repertory of the manners and customs and ideas of the past.

Many of the sayings of the Mishna are expressly ascribed to well-known teachers, and we may fairly suppose that within certain limits the ascription is correct. It is not too much to suppose that sayings might be transmitted with fair accuracy from the time of Christ to the end of the second century. People would be more scrupulous about altering the sayings of Gamaliel than they would be in modifying an anonymous tradition. Where the teachers in question lived later than Christ, the probability that their words are accurately reported is increased, and yet it is not likely that they are essentially different from previous teaching. Much of the Mishna is anonymous, and no doubt received its present form from Rabbi Judah, or those who somewhat later put the Mishna into its present state. Here too there must have been some development since the time of Christ, but such development by no means robs the Mishna of its value as illustrating the New Testament. What took place was not alteration but development, and that development not of any new features of Judaism, nor yet of any spiritual or esoteric teaching; but of the elaborate

THE GOSPELS GENERALLY.

ceremonial and oppressive formalism that Christ continually denounced. Possibly slight tendencies that in the time of Christ could only be discerned by a prophetic instinct, by the time of the Mishna had asserted themselves in evident law and custom. We may understand the tendencies all the better by studying them in a later stage, the full-grown tree may help us to understand the sapling.

Both the Gospel and the Mishna were written in a sense without bias. Jost says of the Mishna that it is not written to support a teacher or a party, nor is it written to prove any particular views of truth, but its object is to preserve practical truth felt to be important. Probably any candid reader will agree with Jost in this, and might even go further and own that only the strictest sense of duty would have induced anyone to undertake so laborious and monotonous a task. Nor can one believe that Rabbi Judah expected that the Mishna would attract anyone to the doctrines or the practice of Judaism. *Absence of bias.*

Thus the Mishna has a special value for the illustration of the Gospels, because we are sure that it has not been adapted to the Gospels. When we read in early Christian writers of Jewish manners and customs illustrating the New Testament we are sometimes tempted to suspect that the illustrations have been invented or modified to suit that which is to be illustrated, but no such suspicion is possible in the case of a Jewish book, handed down by Jews.

There are indeed two tendencies which detract from our confidence in the historical accuracy of the Mishna. One of these is the very natural desire to emphasise the former glory of the nation and this leads to exaggeration. In some cases the exaggeration is obvious, especially where it strays *Tendency to exaggerate former glory.*

26   THE MISHNA AS ILLUSTRATING

into the region of the absurdly supernatural. For instance we must attribute the statement[1] that the opening of the gate of the Temple was heard at Jericho rather to patriotic imagination than to accurate memory. In other cases where the Mishna enlarges on the wonders and magnificence of the former dispensation we may consider that there is fair ground for suspicion. However to illustrate the Gospels we have rather to attend to what is said of the sin and folly of the Jews, we are not so much concerned with the splendour of the Temple services.

<small>Tendency to invent details.</small> There is also the tendency to invent details. Anyone who is familiar with modern commentators knows how upon one or two vague hints and upon the very silence of the narrative an ingenious and learned critic will build up a complete biography of a man of whom really nothing is known but the name. A more imaginative and poetic age invented with greater boldness and the necessary terseness of oral tradition would soon convert conjecture into statement. We can scarcely help believing that as new exigencies arose, new rules to meet them were supplied at times from an artificially stimulated memory and that gaps in antiquarian records would be supplied by the imagination.

There are however limits within which these disturbing forces do not act. In the Mishna and the Gospel we have two independent witnesses, witnesses too that are in the main honest; the Mishna rather exaggerates than perverts. They are independent, neither has been modified so as either to confirm or contradict the other. Hence where they agree we have the coincidence of two independent witnesses, and

[1] Tamid III. 8.

such agreement is always acknowledged to afford a strong presumption of the truth of both.

If too either of our authorities explains the other, either the Mishna the Gospel, or the Gospel the Mishna, such explanation also is a sign of accuracy in both. A clumsy mistake is often obscure, and may become obscurer every time it is repeated, but one clumsy mistake cannot explain another. Again an obscurity which arises out of a mistake may be explained and made to seem accurate by statements specially concocted with a view to their bearing on the mistake. But no one would suspect the Mishna of aiming at making clear what is obscure in the Gospels. For instance the Mishna tells us that there was a golden vine[1] over the doorway of the Temple; we at once think of the parable of the vine, and are perhaps willing to believe that the parable was suggested by this vine. If so the Gospel narrative would be made more vivid for us. We are at any rate sure that the record of the parable and the statement in the Mishna are independent and we feel that in some degree the undesigned coincidence is a proof in favour of the authority of both the Jewish and the Christian witness.

There is, however, another tendency in the Mishna which needs to be taken into account. The Jewish Rabbis seem to have been possessed by a sort of antiquarian enthusiasm for the study of obsolete laws. A recent Jewish writer says[2]: *Antiquarian interest of the Rabbis in obsolete laws.*

'They studied with as much zeal the laws concerning the perverse and rebellious son, which according to the Talmud were never applied, as those which were in daily use'.

---

[1] Middoth III. 8.
[2] Klein, *La Vérité sur le Talmud*, p. 14.

28 THE MISHNA AS ILLUSTRATING THE GOSPELS GENERALLY.

Very different results might spring from this tendency; on the one hand this antiquarian interest would preserve the memory of manners and customs that might else have been forgotten. On the other hand we cannot be certain that manners and customs treated of at length in the Mishna were not obsolete even before the time of Christ. We are told that the use of the Waters of Jealousy was done away with by a contemporary of Christ, and yet the whole subject is discussed at great length and in minute detail in the section Sota. These academic discussions on obsolete law could not be checked or controlled by the necessity of practically applying the decisions arrived at. Hence it is likely that many of the cases dealt with are mere subtleties of theory, and never had any counterpart in the actual life of the Jews.

Summary. Recurring to our original question as to how far the customs, feelings and doctrines of the Jews as given in the Mishna are similar to those of the Jews in the time of Christ. We have said already above that in substance and spirit the position of the Jews in the Mishna is that of the Jews of the first century after Christ. We may now add that in some cases we may use the Mishna as a diagram on a large scale of somewhat microscopic tendencies in the Jews of the Gospel, and that details wherein both coincide or wherein the one explains the other may fairly be considered accurate. Beyond this our ground is very uncertain, and the estimate of the value of the Mishna as representing Jewish life in the time of Christ will depend very much on subjective considerations.

CHAPTER IV.

THE PHARISEES.

IN making use of the Mishna, we have to ask which side Mishna of Jewish life or which party in Jewish teaching or politics, Pharisees. as they existed in the time of Christ, the Mishna represents? The Gospels recognise Herodians, Sadducees and Pharisees; Josephus adds Essenes. As will be seen later on, the teaching of the Mishna connects itself with that of the Pharisees, variously described as Pharisees, scribes and teachers of the law[1].

We next ask how far the Rabbis of the Mishna resembled the Pharisees, how far in recounting the traditions of earlier times they acknowledge or imply that their predecessors the Pharisees correctly held and worthily represented the teaching of their tradition?

It is true that we find in the Mishna and Gemara half contemptuous satire and even direct attack on the Pharisees.

---

[1] νομοδιδάσκαλοι. Not all Pharisees would be scribes or teachers of the law, but these two latter classes seem included in the party of the Pharisees.

'The wounds of a Pharisee' incurred according to the commentators in his anxiety to avoid looking at a woman, 'are among the things that overthrow the world[1]'. Elsewhere, however, the views of Sadducees and Pharisees are discussed with a marked preference[2] for those of the Pharisees, and the authorities quoted in the Mishna are mostly known as Pharisees[3].

Besides this the Mishna mostly either coincides with or is in harmony with what we know of the teaching of the Pharisees. It does not speak of its traditions definitely as those of the Pharisees, nor does it speak of them as differing from Pharisaic teaching.

Probably even in our Lord's time the leading teachers were far from countenancing all the extravagancies of their followers. And then as time went on the nomenclature of parties would change. The Jewish teachers are not spoken of in the Mishna as Pharisees but as Rabbis, and collectively as 'the Sages'. And the 'Chaberim[4]', or 'Associates', are spoken of as careful observers of the Oral Law as distinguished from the 'Am-Ha-Arez[5], who seem to have been very lax in their observance. Probably the more intelligent teachers dropped the title Pharisee, and the more old-fashioned clung to it and exaggerated in their conduct some of the more objectionable features of Pharisaic practice. Those of the party who had adopted new names, and as it were a new dress, might feel some contempt for those who affected the old costume[6]. This feeling, together with

---

[1] Sota III. 4.   [2] Yadaim II. 6, 7, 8.
[3] e. g. Simon, son of Gamaliel. *Vita Josephi*, § 38.
[4] חברים.   [5] עם הארץ.
[6] Cf. the slighting way in which some Radicals speak of Whigs.

some censure of leaders on unworthy followers, and possibly an element of playful self-satire, may account for the critical remarks of the Mishna on the Pharisees, without assuming any vital difference of opinion between the two parties.

We may say therefore that Christ, in His controversies with the Pharisees, came into contact with the principles expressed in the Mishna. What then were the relations between Christ and the Pharisees? We find Him as a lad in the temple seeking to understand them and their teaching. He arouses in them curiosity and astonishment. Later on they and their emissaries follow closely and watch carefully both John the Baptist and Christ. At last they decided against both[1]. Herod relieved them of any anxiety as to John; but they were left to compass the ruin of Christ for themselves. From the time of their decision their opposition became more bitter and more conspicuous, and was probably not lessened by the conversion of Nicodemus and other Pharisees and rulers. The Pharisees of the Synoptists and the corresponding 'Jews'[2] of S. John's Gospel meet Christ at every turn with carping criticism and insidious plots, and throughout the Gospels they are scarcely ever mentioned by Christ except to be condemned.

Herein lies a difficulty, the Christian reader of the Mishna is tempted to look upon the book as a literary Antichrist and to consider it his duty to find there nothing but falsehood and folly as exemplified by the sins and vices of the Pharisees.

It is not difficult to find such, but it must be remembered

Christ and Pharisees.

[1] John ix. 24, &c.; Luke xx. 5.
[2] Westcott on the Gospel of St John. Introduction I. i. i. a.

that the popular manifestation and application of the teaching of the schools often exaggerates its worst points. Christ would largely come in contact with such popular Pharisaism. Among the Pharisees there may have been men as different from the fanatics whom Christ denounces as Cardinal Newman is from some ignorant Catholic priest or as Matthew Arnold is from ignorant and violent sceptics. Between the time of Christ and that of Judah the Holy the Jews had undergone the discipline of severe suffering, and many of the teachers quoted in the Mishna had been martyrs and confessors of their faith. All sects have their striving after truth and holiness, the Pharisees and the Rabbis are no exception. The Rabbis of the time of the Mishna were probably of a somewhat higher type than the popular Pharisee of the Gospel.

The Scribes and Pharisees sit in Moses' seat, their teaching is to be observed, 'these ought ye to have done', but the example of their life is to be avoided. Christ and the Pharisees clash on the importance of forms, it is not so much that the Pharisees challenge His general teaching or that He condemns altogether their forms in themselves, but He challenges their slavery to form and they His neglect of form. Moreover an attack on a system must be practically on its incarnation in the life of a people, wherein oftentimes the better features of a system are lost or have so little influence that it scarcely falls within the province of a reformer to notice them.

We may now proceed to illustrate from the Mishna some of those peculiarities of the Pharisees which are so well known from the Gospels. On some more important matters we will treat more at length in separate chapters, but it

THE PHARISEES. 33

will be convenient to group under this head many of our illustrations on minor points.

These peculiarities of the Pharisees may be summed up in formalism, exclusiveness and hypocrisy.

(i) *Formalism*: consisting in an excessive devotion to a multiplicity of forms, many of them very minute. One leading instance of this devotion is found in their attitude to the Sabbath, but this we reserve for a special chapter. *Formalism.*

Another instance is their scrupulous attention to legal purity. On one occasion they assail the disciples and on another Christ Himself for not washing before a meal. We read in the same connection of their frequent washings of pots and vessels, and of their carefulness as to 'meats[1]'. *Legal Purity.*

To this subject of legal purifications is devoted that one of the six great divisions of the Mishna called the Seder Taharoth. This division contains twelve treatises, and of these there are four which deal with 'Vessels', 'Liquors', 'Hands', 'Stalks', respectively.

The treatise Yadaim or 'Hands' contains regulations for purifying the hands from uncleanness. Maimonides in his commentary on this treatise[2] tells us that the custom of washing the hands before meals was instituted by the scribes, when or by whom is doubtful. The object was to make sure that the hands should not be unclean and so render the food unclean, and for greater security the hands were always to be washed before meals even when it was not known that any uncleanness had been incurred. [3]A quarter of a log of water is to be poured on the hands. It must be poured

[1] Matt. xv. 2, xxiii. 25; Mark vii. 2—4; Luke xi. 38.
[2] See Lightfoot, *Horæ Hebraicæ*, on Matt. xv. 2.
[3] For what follows on this subject, see Yadaim.

B. 3

out of a vessel and not from another man's hand; it must not have a bad smell nor have been used for any other purpose; but anyone may pour water upon another man's hands, even an idiot or an ape.

If a man pours water on one hand first and before pouring water on the other rubs the two together, the one hand again becomes unclean. The marginal rendering of the Revised Version of Mark vii. 3[1] is supported by the references of this treatise to the practice of washing the hands up to the wrists.

The hands might be rendered unclean if merely put inside a house infected with leprosy. The question was said to have arisen as to whether they did not become unclean if put in the empty space of an unclean vessel. Moreover they were rendered unclean by touching any portion of the canonical scriptures. This last was an artificial regulation to prevent the careless handling of sacred books. It might seem to us more reasonable if they had been required to wash their hands *before* touching their Bible. We are told that persons who ate with unwashen hands were troubled with a particular class of devils[2]. Rabbi Akiba, when in prison and suffering from thirst, used what little water was at his disposal to wash his hands before prayer[3].

The treatise Kelim or 'Vessels' discusses at great length the liability of vessels of different kinds to contract uncleanness; what precise closeness of contact, with what precise amount of an unclean thing will render vessels unclean; how far the tendency to uncleanness is affected by a vessel having rims, or handles, and many other questions

---

[1] πυγμῇ, 'up to the elbow'.
[2] Lightfoot on Matt. xv. 2.
[3] Jost, Bk. XII. ch. 12.

of like importance. As the law lays down[1] that a vessel contracting legal impurity is to be washed; it is easy to see that as the cases of legal impurity were multiplied so would be the washings.

The treatises 'Maksheerin' and 'Oozekin', 'Liquids' and 'Stalks', deal with the legal purity of food.

'Maksheerin' is an expansion of Leviticus xi. 38, 'But if any water be put upon the seed, and any part of their carcase fall thereon, it shall be unclean'. The question is discussed as to what liquids when 'put upon' grain or herbs render it liable to become unclean. The list extended amongst other things to dew and honey.

'Oozekin' lays down the rule that if the stalk or shell of fruit touch anything unclean, the uncleanness is communicated to the fruit and vice versâ.

Fasting was general in those days, the prophetess Anna fasted, both the disciples of John and the Pharisees fasted often, and Christ Himself sanctions the practice[2].

Fasting.

There is a treatise 'Taanith' or 'Fasting', which is largely taken up with the subject from which it is named. It alludes to the yearly fasts but dwells specially on the arrangements for fasts in case of calamity. A cumulative system is prescribed in case of drought, fasts of increasing severity were to be observed till either the rain came or the harvest was hopelessly spoilt. It may be noticed that while Christ commands the faster[3] to anoint his head and wash his face, the Mishna[4] says that 'During the week in which

[1] Leviticus xi. 32, 33.
[2] Luke ii. 37, v. 33; Matt. vi. 16, 17.
[3] Matt. vi. 17.
[4] Taanith iv. 7. On the 9th of Ab a fast was held in memory of the destruction of the Temple.

36   THE PHARISEES.

Tithes.

the 9th of Ab happens it is prohibited to a person to shave himself or to wash his clothes'.

Two references are made in the Gospels to the minute care with which the Pharisees paid their tithes; in Matthew xxiii. 23 they are spoken of as 'paying tithes of mint and anise and cummin'; and in the parable of the Pharisee and the Publican, the Pharisee makes it his special boast that he pays tithes of all he possesses.

Three treatises in the Mishna deal with the question of tithes.

The treatise Maaseroth and Maaser Sheni are on what are called the First and Second Tithes respectively[1].

The general law of tithes is laid down thus: 'Everything that is eaten and is kept and has increase from the earth is liable to tithes[2]'. That is to say, everything that grows out of the earth and is edible and is of sufficient value to be kept. It is plain that this general definition would include 'mint and anise and cummin'. Lightfoot in his *Horæ Hebraicæ* on Matthew xxiii. 23 quotes from the Mishna passages in which each of these herbs is spoken of as liable to tithes or other legal dues. He also quotes the Talmud Babli to the effect that the tithing of herbs was instituted by the Rabbis. He proceeds thus, "This tithing was added by the Scribes and yet it was approved of by Christ, when He says 'These things ought ye not to leave undone'. Hearken to this, thou who dost not believe in tithes[3]".

The treatise Maaseroth gives long lists of articles to be

---

[1] These tithes are the subject of much controversy, but the question belongs to the Old Testament and not to the New.
[2] Maaseroth I. 1.
[3] 'Audi hoc, ô anti-decimarie.'

tithed, and of the circumstances under which they are or are not liable for tithes.

For instance; a man brings figs into his house, presumably from his own garden and untithed, his children and household servants may eat them without breaking the law; workmen whom he employs may eat of them also, *unless he finds them in food*[1].

Again, when the time of tithing draws near a man must not sell his fruit to anyone who cannot be trusted to pay tithe upon it[2]. It is further laid down[3] that if a man finds a vessel with the letter Mem (*m*) on it, he is to consider this tithe and hand it over to the proper authorities, because presumably Mem is put as the initial of *Maaser*, tithe. Rabbi José however seems not to concur in this decision and suggests that the Mem may be the initial of a man's name.

But the strictness of the Pharisees on the subject of tithes is most forcibly shown by the treatise Demai.

This treatise discusses the case of a strict Jew, who finds himself in possession of that which should have been tithed, but, as far as he knows, may not have been tithed. For the purposes of this treatise the people are divided into Chaberim or Associates, who strictly observe the law, and the 'Am HaArez or common people, who do not. It is laid down that if the former buy titheable articles from the latter, they cannot depend upon the 'Am HaArez having paid tithe and so must pay tithe themselves. Also the Chaber is to be exceedingly careful that he does not lead others to eat that which has not been tithed. If he is carrying herbs and wishes to throw some away to lighten his burden he must

[1] Maaseroth III. 1.   [2] Maaseroth v. 3.
[3] Maaser Sheni IV. 11.

not do so without tithing them, lest any one finding them should eat them untithed. If he find fruit by the wayside and takes it up to eat it and changes his mind he must not throw it away without tithing it[1].

It is evident that the same or even greater caution will be needful in the case of that which is purchased from a Samaritan or a heathen. He that buys wine from Cuthæans[2] is to say: 'The two logs I am going to put aside are for heave offering and ten for tithe and nine for second tithe, and then he may begin to drink'.

Exclusiveness.
(ii) *Exclusiveness.* This feature of the Pharisaïc character is implied in their name, which signifies 'separated'. They withdrew within narrowing circles, shutting out from their fellowship first Gentiles, then Samaritans, then the common people.

Gentiles.
As the scene of action of the Gospels is almost exclusively in Palestine, Christ is scarcely brought into contact with the Gentiles. However it is recorded that a significant reference to the exceptional favour showed to Gentiles like Naaman the Syrian and the widow of Zarephath called forth the indignation of the Jews, who heard it, and no doubt when Christ said to the Syrophenician woman 'Is it meet to cast the children's bread to the dogs?', He wished to remind her how an earnest orthodox Jewish teacher would have viewed her request. In the Acts the idea that Jews must not eat with Gentiles has its influence in the Christian Church.

It is evident that the regulations for legal purity would

---

[1] Demai ɪɪɪ. 2, 3.
[2] i. e. Samaritan and possibly sometimes Gentile. Lightfoot, *Horæ Hebr.* on John iv. 1; Matt. x. 5.

prevent the Jews from free intercourse with Gentiles, and especially from eating with them. Besides this it was necessary to avoid any implication in their idolatry. Rules as to intercourse with idolaters are laid down in the treatise Abodah Zarah: "Three days before the feasts of the idolaters it is forbidden to deal with them, to lend to them or borrow from them, to pay them, to take payment of them. Rabbi Judah said, 'It is allowed to take payment from them, since it is disagreeable to the idolater'. The Sages answered him 'Though it is disagreeable to him now, he rejoices afterwards[1]'".

The object of these restrictions would be to avoid having any share in providing for a heathen festival. It is interesting to notice that authorities are agreed on the desirability of annoying the heathen, though they differ as to the most effectual method.

Again it is said, 'Men must not let to them buildings in the land of Israel and it is needless to say fields[2]'. 'No man should be alone with them, because they are apt to shed blood[3]'. In these rules there is a spirit of suspicious exclusiveness, but it is only too certain that there was much to justify such a spirit.

In the matter of wine the Israelites were much hampered in their dealings with the heathen. The Jew felt that if he drank from a barrel or pitcher of wine, from which a libation had been poured out to an idol, that he was implicated in an act of idolatrous worship. Hence such decisions as these: 'A man dines with an idolater and leaves a flask of wine on the table and one on the sideboard, and left them and went out. The

[1] Abodah Zarah I, 1.   [2] Abodah Zarah I. 10.
[3] Abodah Zarah II. 1.

flask on the table is forbidden to be used, but that on the sideboard is allowed'[1]. This must be explained thus; the absence of the Jew gives the idolater an opportunity of pouring out a libation to some idol-God without the Jew knowing of it; so that the Jew if he drank out of that flask, may be drinking wine from which a libation has been offered. But it is supposed the Jew is not away long enough to give the idolater an opportunity of pouring a libation from the flask on the sideboard and therefore that wine may be used.

Similarly[2], 'If foreign robbers have entered into a city in time of peace, no barrel of wine which was open at the time may be used' because the foreigners may have poured libations from them.

It will be plain from such instances how difference of habits and mutual suspicion together with the anxiety of the Jew to be legally clean and his hatred of idolatry would bring about and find expression for a spirit of rigid exclusiveness in the case of Gentiles.

Samaritans. In the case of the Samaritans the common element of Jewish and Samaritan religion would at times draw them together, but oftener tend to embitter the dislike and suspicion derived from their differences. Religious animosity is acknowledged to be most bitter when the disputants have much in common.

There are in the Gospels several instances of mutual hatred between Jews and Samaritans.

Christ Himself seems to recognise that for practical purposes the Samaritans are on the same level as the Gentiles and that it is necessary to exclude them for the present

---

[1] Abodah Zarah v. 3.
[2] Abodah Zarah, v. 4.

from His work. In sending forth the Twelve[1] He bids them not to go in the way of the Gentiles nor to enter into any city of the Samaritans'. Three times Samaritans are spoken of in a way that seems to imply special reproach to the Jews. In the case of the 'Woman of Samaria'[2], the 'Good Samaritan'[3], and the solitary leper out of the ten healed of whom it is recorded 'and he was a Samaritan'[4], there underlies the narrative a consciousness of the contempt and hatred felt by the Jews for the Samaritans. 'If these Samaritans whom you hate and despise surpass you in faith and good works, ought you not to be ashamed alike of yourselves and of your hatred?' When the Jews want to vent their spleen upon Christ to the uttermost, the worst they can find to say about Him is that 'He is a Samaritan and has a devil'[5].

In one instance we have an illustration of the hatred felt by the Samaritans, for on His last journey from Galilee they would not receive Him because His face was as if He were going to Jerusalem[6].

Later on circumstances somewhat mitigated their mutual hatred. During the Jewish war of Titus and Vespasian, the Samaritans assembled in arms and seemed about to revolt, but were forthwith crushed by the Romans[7]. Common danger and common suffering seem for a time to have brought about a partial reconciliation between Jews and Samaritans, but when danger and suffering gave place again to peace and security the old hatred and jealousy were renewed[8].

The Mishna, being compiled at a time when feeling

---

[1] S. Matt. x. 5.   [2] S. John iv.   [3] S. Luke x.
[4] S. Luke xvii.   [5] S. John viii. 48.   [6] S. Luke ix.
[7] Joseph. *B. J.* III. 7. 32.   [8] Jost, Bk. XIII. Ch. VIII.

had passed through these various phases, bears traces of them all.

We read of ancient acts of hostility on the part of the Samaritans. How the news of the appearance of the new moon used to be communicated by beacon-fires on the mountains. But the Samaritans kindled misleading fires on the wrong days and the practice had to be given up[1].

If an Israelite says grace the rest must say Amen, but if a Samaritan says grace the rest must only say Amen if they have heard the whole of the blessing[2]. An Israelite might safely say Amen to any grace of an Israelite, but a Samaritan grace might contain something heterodox or even blasphemous.

All legal documents, on which the attestation of a Samaritan witness appears, are void, bills of divorce and deeds of manumission excepted[3]. These rules point to a certain intimacy of intercourse between Jews and Samaritans, but also to much suspicion on the part of the Jews as to the honesty of the Samaritans. The latter regulation may possibly be due rather to anxiety that no technical informality should stand in the way of divorce or the manumission of slaves rather than to any confidence in the honesty of Samaritans in these special cases.

Other sayings of the Mishna point to a more irreconcilable hatred and a more complete separation between the two peoples. It is said of the daughter of a Sadducee who treads in her father's footsteps that she is no better than a Samaritan[4]. A saying which reminds us of the Pharisees' taunt 'Thou art a Samaritan'.

[1] Rosh Hashanah II. 2.
[2] Berachoth VIII. 8.
[3] Gittin I. 5.
[4] Niddah IV. 2.

Rabbi Eliezer says that he who eats the bread of the Samaritans is as he who eats swine's flesh[1].

We next have to show how far a spirit of exclusiveness divided the Pharisees or more strictly orthodox Jews from various classes of their own countrymen. Am HaArez.

We are familiar with their attitude towards 'Publicans and sinners'. The crime of the former consisted partly in their being the officers of a foreign power, and so the hatred of the Publican is partly hatred of the foreigner.

The Pharisees come to the disciples with the indignant enquiry 'Why eateth your Master with Publicans and sinners'?[2] Christ Himself says that 'The Son of Man' was called 'a gluttonous man and a wine-bibber, a friend of Publicans and sinners'[3].

In the Mishna Publicans are classed with murderers and other bad characters as persons to whom vows need not be fulfilled[4]. Money coming from Publicans was not to be received that alms might be given from it[5]. A house is unclean if a Publican enters it[6].

While it seemed a patriotic duty to stand aloof from the Publican, enthusiasm for orthodoxy divided them somewhat from the Sadducees. In the Gospels this opposition scarcely comes into notice. Christ and His teaching seem to have been objectionable to both parties. In the Acts however their differences tempted S. Paul to seek for safety from their dissensions[7].

As has been already said the Mishna accepts the views of the Pharisees and mentions those of the Sadducees in

---

[1] Shebiith VIII. 10. [2] S. Matt. ix. 11. [3] S. Matt. xi. 19.
[4] Nedarim III. 4. [5] Baba Kama x. 1.
[6] Taharoth VII. 6. [7] Acts xxiii. 6—8.

order to make light of them and reject them. Since the Sadducee did not accept the oral law there was a danger that vessels might be rendered unclean by his presence[1]. The method prescribed for the preparation of the ashes of the red heifer, involved an undignified skipping on the part of a ram which was employed. Rabbi José said 'You should not give the Sadducees an opportunity for scoffing'[2]. Thus with the Pharisees the Sadducee represents the 'enemy' who will take advantage of any 'occasion to blaspheme'.

From such facts as these as well as from the well-known doctrinal differences, we come to understand that it was no ordinary hatred towards Christ and no slight sense of danger that united parties having so little sympathy one with the other.

We pass on to the attitude of the Pharisees towards the common people. If a Pharisee could have been brought to understand the state of things now-a-days, he would probably have felt that the 'common people' corresponded more or less to the 'lapsed masses'. Even in times when rigid orthodoxy is dominant and strictness of life strenuously insisted on, there is always a large class who admit with reluctance the necessity of the orthodox religious observances and do not pretend to carry them out with any degree of thoroughness. Now it was just this 'common people' who heard Christ gladly, while the Pharisees enquired indignantly 'Have any of the rulers or of the Pharisees believed on Him'? The support given to Christ by the common people was easily disposed of, 'This mob that knoweth not the law is cursed'[3].

[1] Erubin IV. 2. [2] Parah III. 3.
[3] S. John vii. 47—49.

The Mosaic Law invested the person of the priest with a special sanctity and imposed upon him special and additional rules with a view to his legal purity. The Mishna distinguishes different grades of sanctity within the priesthood and divides the people into Pharisees and Am HaArez, the latter corresponding roughly to the 'common people' of the Gospels. Contact with the garments of one of the Am HaArez defiles the Pharisee; contact with the garments of the Pharisee defiles those who eat the heave-offering; contact with the garments of those who eat the heave-offering defiles for eating holy flesh; contact with garments of those who eat the holy flesh defiles for the sin-offering[1].

As has been said already the Pharisees were not allowed to assume that the 'common people' had paid their tithes, so that they could scarcely eat with them for fear they should be eating that which had not paid tithe. If they bought of the 'common people' they had to pay tithe on what they bought.

All these restrictions would limit freedom of intercourse between the Pharisees and the 'common people' and tend to do away with any sympathy between them. The exclusiveness of the Pharisees in different instances may be assigned to different causes; in the case of Gentiles and Publicans to national pride; in the case of the Sadducees to pride of orthodoxy; in the case of the 'common people' pride of learning and of social position; but in all these cases allied with the special causes there was the one dominant cause, the necessity for legal purity.

[1] Hagiga II. 7. To eat of the various offerings was a privilege of the priests and their dependents.

46 THE PHARISEES.

Hypocrisy.

(iii) *Hypocrisy.* We have taken this for a title under which to group some of the characteristics of the Pharisees, because hypocrisy is always spoken of as one of their chief faults, and Christ Himself addresses them as 'hypocrites'. It is probable that the application of the English word in its ordinary acceptation to the Pharisees is misleading. The conventional idea of a hypocrite is that of a man who does not mean what he says and yet says it with the intention and in the hope that people may believe him, and of a man who tries to appear good and to get credit for being so while he lives as wickedly as he can without being found out. In this sense of the word there is very little deliberate hypocrisy, and of conscious hypocrisy there is even less. The conscious stage of hypocrisy is very transient, for it is essential to hypocrisy as to all forms of deceit that sooner or later and for the most part sooner the deceiver deceives himself. Especially there is seldom to any great extent deliberate and conscious hypocrisy on the part of a class. For it is an established law of general morality that a man's own class, who for him are the one source of public opinion, may decree that certain words and phrases are to be understood in a sense different from their ordinary meaning or are to be understood as meaning nothing at all. When this is the case the individual feels that he cannot be charged with hypocrisy for using words thus.

So in the days when the religion of Rome had lost its hold on the educated classes, Cicero and Seneca went through religions and ceremonies and pronounced religious formulæ and had no consciousness of hypocrisy, because everybody, that is everybody worth considering, every educated man, understood that such ceremonies and formulæ were partly a political expedient and partly a meaningless farce. But it may be doubted whether the Pharisees used formulæ and ceremonies they did not believe in. Their hypocrisy was rather one of life and conduct than of words. They professed to follow after holiness and to carry it out into all the minute details of life. Their hypocrisy consisted in the fact that with them holiness of form and ritual had become largely dissociated from holiness of character, justice, mercy and love; their control of minute details broke down in many points, and instead of frankly admitting their incapacity to deal, by means of precise rules, with all the exigencies of life, they strove to hide their failure with the quibbles and evasions of a feeble and dishonest casuistry.

At first sight this may seem far too mild a statement of the case against the Pharisees. Christ seems to accuse them of open immorality, they are devourers of widows' houses, full of extortion and excess. He accuses them of utter hypocrisy in religion, it is for a pretence that they make long prayers. He sums up their character by calling them 'children of the devil'—'children of Gehenna'. Surely Lightfoot is right when he says that 'the best of the Pharisees would be certainly the worst of men'?[1]

But a man might be guilty of all the sins with which Christ charges the Pharisees and yet not be considered either by himself or by others disreputable or irreligious. There have been in all ages legal and respectable ways of devouring widows' houses. A profession of special interest in particular religious views may be believed to be due to political or ecclesiastical partisanship and yet those who

[1] *Horæ Hebr.* on Matt. III. 7, optimi Pharisaeorum, certe pessimi hominum.

make the profession are not scouted as hypocrites. Great preachers in days when plain speaking was more in fashion have addressed congregations in language almost as strong as that used by Christ of and to the Pharisees. As for their murder of Christ it was to them simply a political necessity; Christian prelates and sovereigns usually cut short the career of obnoxious religious teachers much more promptly. The special misfortune of the Pharisees that has made their name a by-word was that their formalism and insincerity were contrasted with the simple earnestness and straightforward honesty of Christ.

Crimes doubtless the Pharisees as individuals were guilty of, and probably their peculiar system had much to do in determining them to such crimes; but it would be as useless to look in the Mishna for the authorisation of wholesale robbery, fraud and hypocrisy as such, as it would be to seek in the canons of the Church of Rome for any official justification of the murders of Borgia or the vices of his cardinals.

Having thus tried to guard against an over-estimate of the sins of Pharisees, we may point out certain traces of these sins which are to be found in the Mishna. Christ charges the Pharisees with insincerity in their religious observances, with avarice and with an undue thirst for social and scholastic preëminence. Insincerity in religious observance, making long prayers for a pretence, fasting and giving alms that men may see and admire, these faults are the natural outcome of that excessive formalism already noticed. It inculcated the observance of a multiplicity of forms, it laid stress on the observance of these forms while little or nothing is said as to their inner or spiritual meaning. It became easy to forget that there was any meaning and forms of prayer and worship might be treated like the incantations of a magician. If a multiplicity of forms was an essential of religion, he who observed most forms surpassed others in religion, and he who desired a reputation for holiness was tempted to make an extensive display of such observances, without any reference to real worship.

For instance, in the matter of Prayers, there is a treatise called 'Blessings' which lays down minute rules as to prayers. It was the duty of men among the Israelites to repeat morning and evening the Shema, i.e. the passage beginning 'Hear, O Israel, the Lord our God is one Lord'[1]. Exact rules are laid down as to the times from which and up to which the Shema may be said; also as to whether it is to be said standing or reclining, whether it may be said on the top of a tree or on a wall. Later on the question of 'Blessings' is discussed at length. After eating figs, grapes and pomegranates three blessings must be said according to Rabban Gamaliel, but according to the Wise Men only one. He who sees a place where signs were wrought for Israel is to say 'Blessed be He who wrought signs for our fathers in this place'. On comets, earthquakes, lightnings, thunder and tempests, a man is to say 'Blessed be He whose strength and might fill the world'. Many other such blessings are given, so that in many places and on many occasions the strict Jew would have an opportunity of displaying his careful obedience. Here and there in this mass of minute rules something is said that might suggest the necessity of earnestness and sincerity in prayer; it is said 'Man is bound

---

[1] Christ speaks of this as the first of all the commandments, S. Mark xii. 29.

to bless God for evil, as he is bound to bless Him for good'. It is said elsewhere 'When thou prayest, make not thy prayer an ordinance, but an entreaty before God[1]', which is thus explained: 'Prayer is not to be said merely at set times and as a duty, but is to be the expression of a heartfelt desire[2]'.

It may not be fair to measure the relative interest felt by the Rabbis in the forms and in the spirit of prayer by the space they devote to these several subjects; but it is certain that people in general would pay more attention to the copious directions as to the form than to the very occasional sayings on the spirit, and the result would be insincerity.

It is also said of the Pharisees that they were avaricious[3]. Possibly the Mishna does not directly and specially illustrate the avarice of the Pharisees. It is difficult to see on what grounds rules could be laid down which should secure special pecuniary advantages for a particular sect or school of religious thought. But from the close connection in the Gospels and elsewhere between priests and Pharisees we gather that the priests were mostly of the Pharisaic party[4], and so the Pharisees in caring for the interests of the priests would be consulting their own interests. The Mishna is very careful of the interests of the priests, it enforces the payment of the tithes which they were to receive and also

---

[1] Pirke Aboth II. 17.
[2] Taylor, *Sayings of the Jewish Fathers*, p. 52.
[3] Luke xvi. 14.
[4] During the period of the Acts, the High Priest and his kindred were Sadducees; but it is not necessary to suppose that their example was followed by the other priests.

of their other dues. The heave-offering if offered by a man living near the priest, so that the offering would not have time to go bad, was to be taken from the best, but otherwise from that which would keep longest[1]. It is said that the rich brought firstfruits in gold and silver baskets which were given to the priests[2]. Moreover the fulfilment of any vow which was to the disadvantage of a priest might be hindered by force[3].

It is easier to find striking illustrations of the appetite of the Rabbis for fame, their tendency to seek honour of men, the first seats at feasts and in the synagogues, greetings in the market place and the salutation 'Rabbi'.

The exhortation 'Get thyself a master' is often repeated in one form or another[4]. Again it is said 'Let the fear of thy master be as the fear of heaven[5]'. The possible arrival of a 'Wise Man' or 'Teacher' is considered likely to be the occasion of special arrangements for going out to meet him on the Sabbath[6]. It is also laid down that he who takes the Nazirite vow in the faith that the Wise Men can absolve him from his vow is to be absolved, but Rabbi Simeon dissents from this decision[7].

We have thus shewn that the picture of the Pharisee as given by the Gospels in its leading features of formalism, exclusiveness and in a special sense hypocrisy is borne out by the Mishna. Other less prominent characteristics, such as

[1] Terumah II. 4.
[2] Bikoorim III. 8.
[3] Nedarim XI. 3.
[4] Pirke Aboth I. 4, 7, 17.
[5] Pirke Aboth IV. 17.
[6] Erubin III. 5.
[7] Nazir II. 4.

their views on divorce and on the resurrection will come more conveniently under other heads. What there is in the Mishna of purer and more spiritual teaching will also be better treated separately.

CHAPTER V.

THE SABBATH.

OF those matters of form and outward observance on which Christ and the Pharisees clashed the Sabbath came into question oftenest, and it was on this point that Christ wounded most deeply the prejudices of the Pharisees.

Out of some thirty-three recorded miracles, seven were wrought on the Sabbath[1]. In two cases only out of the seven, the healing of the demoniac at Capernaum and the healing of Peter's wife's mother, did He fail to excite the severest criticism, and after the healing of the man with the withered hand, the Pharisees planned His death. One of the leading motives of the Pharisees in desiring His death was that He persistently set Himself against the observance of the Sabbath as they understood it.

It is perhaps easiest to state the Pharisaic view of the Sabbath by a slight exaggeration and to say that they held concerning the Sabbath exactly what Christ denied, namely,

Pharisees and Sabbath.

[1] The Healing of the Impotent Man at Bethesda, S. John v. The Demoniac at Capernaum and Simon's Wife's Mother, S. Luke iv. The Withered Hand, S. Luke vi. The Man born Blind, S. John ix. The Woman with a Spirit of Infirmity, S. Luke xiii. The Healing of the Man with a Dropsy, S. Luke xiv.

'That man was made for the Sabbath', and it is interesting to find in the Book of Jubilees[1] the statement that the Sabbath was ordained before the Creation and that Israel was chosen to keep it.

The Sabbath appears to have been for the Pharisees chiefly a day when you must not do things, the things in question being numerous and extending into minute details of life carefully and exhaustively defined. The Fourth Commandment was not supposed to be sufficiently intelligible to ordinary common sense, nor was it interpreted according to the spirit and intention but according to the letter. Moreover while some allowance seems to be made for works of beneficence and necessity, yet this was grudgingly conceded and carefully limited.

Impotent Man. Some of the points on which the Pharisees attack Christ are the veriest trifles. For instance a man carries the rough mat that formed his bed[2], this comes under the head of carrying burdens. Indeed this was no trifle to the Pharisees, for take illustrations of their idea of burdens: milk equal to a mouthful, ink enough to write two letters, paint enough to dye one eye, reed sufficient to make a writing pen, or bone enough to make a spoon[3]. Moreover they discussed carefully what instruments might be carried without being considered burdens. A tailor may not go out with a needle nor a scribe with a pen[4], but a cripple may go out with crutches, though R. Meir and R. José are at issue as to whether he may go out with a wooden leg[5]. It is also a grave question as to where the line is to be drawn between ornaments or articles

---

[1] A Jewish work assigned by different authorities to various dates from 100 B.C. to 100 A.D.
[2] S. John v.
[3] Sabbath VIII.
[4] Sabbath I. 3.
[5] Sabbath VI. 8.

of dress and burdens. A woman may go out with plaits of false hair, but it is a question whether she may go out with a false tooth[1]. A woman may not wear a frontlet on the Sabbath unless it is sewn to her cap[1]. Now a bed, even the rug of the Easterns, was very clearly larger than the reed sufficient to make a pen. It was not an instrument necessary for walking like a crutch, nor yet on any ground an article of dress, to carry it was a clear and gross transgression of the law.

At another time the indignation of the Pharisees was aroused, because the disciples plucked ears of corn on the Sabbath day and rubbed them in their hands[2]. Among the principal works which are forbidden on the Sabbath are reaping, threshing, winnowing, sifting and grinding[3]. There is no exact definition given of these kinds of work as there is of building. It is indeed a question whether a man does not break the Sabbath if he plucks anything from a flower in a pot[4]. It is laid down also that 'Men must not squeeze fruits, so as to extract the juice, and if it ooze out of itself it is forbidden to use it. Rabbi Judah says "If the fruits are for eating, the juice which oozes out may be used, but if the fruits are for beverage, the juice which oozes out is forbidden for use[5]"'.

Plucking ears of corn.

In the light of these restrictions and remembering the way in which the term 'burdens' is understood by the Pharisees, it becomes evident that the disciples had been guilty of a very complicated crime. They had been plucking ears of corn, probably not two or three, but handfuls. This

---

[1] Sabbath vi. 5.
[2] S. Luke vi. and parallel.
[3] Sabbath vii. 2.
[4] Sabbath x. 6.
[5] Sabbath xxii. 1.

was reaping. Then they had rubbed it in their hands, which would be equivalent to winnowing and sifting, and might even be considered an attempt at grinding.

Man born blind.
In healing the man born blind, Christ made clay and anointed his eyes[1]. The making of clay is evidently an important point, for when the man is asked how his eyes were opened he says 'The man called Jesus made clay and anointed my eyes', and the Evangelist is careful to tell us that it was on the Sabbath that Jesus made the clay and opened the man's eyes. This making of clay might be considered kneading, which is another 'principal work' not to be done on the Sabbath. But even as the preparation of a dressing it would be forbidden. For instance a man must not prepare brine on the Sabbath[2]; and though a child may be circumcised on the Sabbath[3], yet if oil and wine have not been already mixed on the Sabbath eve, they must be put on separately; a proper dressing may not be prepared on the Sabbath, but a linen rag may be tied on the wound[4]. Circumcision had to be performed on the eighth day and yet the rules for the Sabbath are only reluctantly and partially set aside: a blind man might receive his sight any day, there was no excuse whatever for preparing a dressing in his case[5].

There remain three other cases in which Christ incurred the censure of the Pharisees by healing on the Sabbath: the healing of the man with the withered hand, the healing of the woman with a spirit of infirmity, and the healing of the man with a dropsy. His guilt in these three cases must

[1] S. John ix. 6.   [2] Sabbath xiv. 2.
[3] Sabbath xix. 2.   [4] Cf. S. John vii. 22, 23.
[5] It has also been pointed out in this connection that at sunset, when the Sabbath ended, sick folk were brought to Christ. Their friends had evidently waited till the Sabbath was over. S. Mark i. 32.

have been simply that He healed the sufferers. It is true that He laid His hands on the afflicted woman and commanded the man with a withered hand to stretch it forth; but it could scarcely be called work or a violation of the Sabbath to touch any one or to stretch forth one's hand.

In all these three cases Christ appeals to the charity and humanity of the Pharisees and points His appeal by reminding them of the works of mercy they permitted in the case of animals. 'What man shall there be of you, that shall have one sheep, and if this fall into a pit on the Sabbath day will he not lay hold on it and lift it out? How much then is a man of more value than a sheep'[1]?

'Hypocrites, doth not each one of you on the Sabbath loose his ox or his ass from the stall and lead him away to watering? And ought not this woman, being a daughter of Abraham, whom Satan had bound, lo, these eighteen years, to have been loosed from this bond on the day of the Sabbath'[2]?

With regard to the raising of an animal from a pit, Lightfoot[3] gives quotations from the Gemara and Maimonides which are not quite consistent. The Gemara says that if a beast and its young fall into a pit, the beast may be taken out with a view to killing it and must be killed, while the young may be supplied with food in the pit. It mentions however that Rabbi Joshua says that the intention of killing the beast need not be carried out and that the young may be taken out. The quotation from Maimonides which is well known from commentaries says that if a beast fall into a pit or pool of water, the owner may give it food, if

---

[1] S. Matt. xii. 11, 12.   Cf. S. Luke xiv. 15.
[2] S. Luke xiii. 15, 16.   [3] *Horæ Hebr. in loco.*

he cannot do this, he may place rags and planks to support it and if these happen to enable the beast to get out, it may get out.

The Mishna itself contains many provisions for the care of cattle on the Sabbath. Straw may be untied for cattle, pumpkins may be cut up for them and carrion for dogs[1]. Men may cleanse the crib for a stalled ox, at least so Rabbi Dosa says, but the Wise Men forbid this. Men may move fodder from before one beast to put it before another on the Sabbath[2]. Also arrangements are made for taking animals to wells on the Sabbath and giving them water[3].

But in spite of these reasonable arrangements for cattle, concessions to men in suffering and sickness are very slight and jealously restricted. He who has toothache must not rinse his teeth with vinegar[4]. He who has pains in his loins must not rub them with wine or vinegar, but may anoint them with oil, except it be rose oil[5]. Anointing with oil it must be remembered was a regular practice and therefore not specially medicine. Men must not close the eyes of the dead on the Sabbath[6]. The priests in the temple may replace a plaster on the Sabbath, but must not do so in the country. It is forbidden either in the temple or in the country to put the first plaster on a wound. A priest, who hurts his finger, may bind it up with reeds in the temple on the Sabbath, but not in the country[7].

Other restrictions. There are other restrictions to which there is no reference in the Gospels. There are numerous rules about the lighting of lamps, the burning of which was regarded as a sacred duty.

[1] Sabbath xxiv. [2] Sabbath xx. 4. [3] Erubin ii. 2.
[4] It is interesting to know that Rabbi Judah himself is said to have been much afflicted with toothache. Jost, Bk. xiii. Ch. x.
[5] Sabbath xiv. 4. [6] Sabbath xxiii. 5. [7] Erubin x. 13, 14.

Of course no cooking may be done on the Sabbath, an egg must not be put by the side of a hot kettle. But the reader may ask how can there be a hot kettle on the Sabbath? A kettle may be boiled on the Sabbath-eve and kept warm under garments or feathers. As man must not pare his nails, a woman must not dye her eyebrows on the Sabbath[1]. Building of course is forbidden. 'He who builds how much must he build to become guilty? Whoever builds at all, whoever chops a stone, strikes with a hammer or uses a plane, or bores a hole'[2].

It is forbidden to write two letters of the alphabet on the Sabbath, or to weave three threads. Labourers must not be hired on the Sabbath. Also there are many other restrictions of no special interest, which are sufficiently illustrated by the above instances.

One great rule as to the Sabbath is the subject of a whole treatise, Erubin, and that treatise is largely an account of expedients by which the strict observance of the rule may be evaded.

Mixtures.

It is written 'Abide ye every man in his place, let no man go out of his place on the seventh day'[3]. A man's place was understood to be the city where he lived together with a belt of country round the city 2000 cubits or about six furlongs broad; so that a man could on the Sabbath start from his house, go to the boundary of the city and proceed further any distance not greater than 2000 cubits.

Again, the last of the thirty-nine 'principal works' which

---

[1] Sabbath x. 6.   [2] Sabbath xii. 1.
[3] Ex. xvi. 29. Originally this seems to have referred to going out of the camp to gather manna, but the Jews held it to be of perpetual obligation.

are forbidden on the Sabbath is the carrying of anything from one house or set of premises[1] to another.

The former rule gave rise to the well-known 'Sabbath Day's Journey'.

The latter is illustrated by the following example: A mendicant stands outside and the master of the house inside the house; should the mendicant put his hand into the house and put anything (possibly his wallet, so RR. de Sola and Raphall) into the master's hand, or take something out of the master's hand and draw his hand back, the mendicant is guilty, but the master of the house is free from blame. Should the master put his hand outside the house and put his gift into the hand of the mendicant, or take the wallet out of it and draw his hand back, the master of the house is guilty, but the mendicant is free from blame. Should the mendicant put his hand inside the house and the master take the wallet out of it or put his gift into it, and the mendicant draw his hand out, both are free from blame. Should the master stretch out his hand and the mendicant take the gift out of it, or put his wallet into it, both are free from blame.

In the first of these four cases the master is entirely passive and the mendicant is the sole agent in transferring a burden from the inside of the house to the outside, and so bears the blame; in the second case the master is the sole agent, and he bears the blame. In the last two cases the act of transfer is divided between the two, neither is guilty of a complete act and neither is to blame.

[1] רְשׁוּת, specially רְשׁוּת הַיָּחִיד, private property: any place surrounded or inclosed by a wall, or a ditch ten hands wide and four deep; also the ditch itself; any city encompassed by walls that are closed at night. Introduction to treatise Sabbath in RR. de Sola and Raphall.

Obviously these two rules would often be very inconvenient. The Sabbath was a day largely devoted to social intercourse, and it might chance that neighbours and friends lived just outside the Sabbath day's journey; or some need might arise for travelling somewhat further on the Sabbath. Then, too, it would often be natural and reasonable that the mistresses of neighbouring houses should lend or borrow and render neighbourly help. This would be impossible without carrying burdens from one house to another, and would therefore be prohibited if the second rule were made absolute and invariable.

In order to afford some relief from the stringency of these rules, recourse was had to the method of Erubin or mixtures. By this method one house was 'mixed' or combined with another so as to form one, and then anything might be carried from house to house; also one Sabbath day's journey was combined with another, and a man was enabled to go 4000 cubits on the Sabbath.

The principle upon which this method is based is that 'where a man's meat is there is his house'. Thus courts are combined by all the householders of the court uniting to place some article of food in a given place, by doing so they, as it were, form themselves into one family, and all the dwellings of the court become for the time one general and common abode for all its inmates, who thereby become entitled to carry and convey from one house to another within the limits of the court on the Sabbath.

He who wishes to combine one Sabbath day's journey with another so as to be able to go two on the Sabbath, must, before the coming in of the Sabbath, deposit food for two meals in any particular place within the original limits of the Sabbath day's journey. This place now becomes his home, he is allowed on the Sabbath to go home and then 2000 cubits beyond it[1]. A man might deposit food in two places and avail himself of whichever suited him. He may say, 'If foes come from the east I will avail myself of my deposit in the west to go westward and flee from them; if they come from the west I will avail myself of my deposit in the east. If they come from both sides I shall go in which direction I please[2]'. There are also conventions by which adjoining towns may be treated as one town.

Accidental transgression of Sabbatical limits. A man who, by any accident, is taken or goes out of the due limit on the Sabbath, finds himself in a very awkward predicament. If foes or an evil spirit have caused a man to go out beyond the Sabbath limit, he must not move further than four cubits. If they have carried him into another town and put him into a prison or fold for cattle, he may, according to Rabban Gamaliel and R. Eleazar ben Azariah, go about throughout its whole extent; but R. Joshua and R. Akiba maintain that he must not move further than four cubits. It once happened that these four Rabbis came together from Parendisim and their vessel kept the sea on the Sabbath (so that they were carried more than the prescribed distance). Rabban Gamaliel and R. Eleazar ben Azariah walked about throughout the whole of the vessel; but R. Joshua and R. Akiba did not move beyond four cubits, as they wished to observe the law with rigid accuracy[3].

Relaxations. We may notice some other slight relaxations of the strict rules of the Sabbath. If a fire occurs on the Sabbath sacred

---

[1] RR. de Sola and Raphall, introduction to treatise Erubin.
[2] Erubin III. 5.   [3] Erubin IV. 1.

writings are to be saved, also food for three meals, also a basket full of loaves, a fig cake, a cask of wine. It is lawful to call to others to save what they can for themselves. A man may carry out all vessels required for his meals that day. He may dress himself in as much as he can put on and gird about him as much as he can. R. José saith he must not put on more than eighteen garments, but he may go back and dress himself in another eighteen and get others to do the same[1]. These expedients enable the man to save his wardrobe and other portions of his property without incurring the guilt of carrying burdens on the Sabbath; for to take up his property and carry it out in a straightforward way would be carrying burdens.

An Israelite may take advantage of work done by a heathen on the Sabbath, provided the work has not been done at his request. For instance, if the heathen comes to put out the fire he is not to be told to extinguish the fire nor yet to be forbidden to do so. The Israelites are not bound to make him keep the Sabbath. If a heathen lights a candle, an Israelite may use the light unless it has been lighted on purpose for the Israelite; if a heathen has drawn water for his cattle to drink, the Israelite may give his cattle to drink after him, unless the water has been drawn on purpose for the Israelite. If a heathen has made a step to descend from a ship, an Israelite may descend after him, unless the heathen made it on purpose for the Israelite. It once happened that Rabban Gamaliel and the elders arrived in a ship, and a heathen made a step by which he descended and Rabban Gamaliel and the elders descended after him[2].

---

[1] Sabbath xvi. [2] Sabbath xvi.

These rules made it obviously convenient to be in the neighbourhood of heathens on the Sabbath day, and ought to have done something to create a kindly feeling on the part of the Israelites toward the heathen. How the feelings of the heathen would be influenced it is difficult to say. Another rule implies much simple trust on the part of the Israelite toward the heathen. It was forbidden to carry money on the Sabbath, so the Israelite who on the Sabbath-eve was overtaken by the dusk on the road was to give his purse to the heathen.

Another principle of the Mishna is that if any work gets done without its being intended to be done advantage may be taken of it. He who has strained his hand or foot must not pour cold water on it; but he may wash it in the usual way; and if he does get cured he does get cured[1]. He who has the toothache must not rinse his teeth with vinegar, but he may wash them as usual, and if he does get cured, he does get cured[2]. It is also laid down that work done unintentionally on the Sabbath may be taken advantage of, but if done intentionally it may not[3].

These regulations pave the way for evasions of the law; a man's interests might lead him to affect ignorance of the motives of the heathen or even forgetfulness of his own intentions. Entirely opposed to this is the fragment found in Codex Bezæ after Luke v. 10 "On the same day seeing a man working on the Sabbath, he said to him: 'Man, if thou knowest what thou art doing happy art thou, but if thou

---

[1] Sabbath XXII. 6. [2] Sabbath XIV. 4.
[3] Terumah II. 3.

knowest not thou art accursed and a transgressor of the law'".

In all this there was the intention of glorifying God by keeping His Sabbath, and in spite of all this heavy burden of Sabbath keeping the day is spoken of as one of repose and enjoyment. For it is said 'They did not fast on the eve of the Sabbath, for honour to the Sabbath. Nor on the first day, that they should not go forth from repose and enjoyment to toil and fasting and death[1]. Moreover we know that feasts were given on the Sabbath. On the Sabbath Christ goes to eat bread at the house of a Pharisee with a company of Pharisees[2]. And yet in spite of all this the Sabbath must have been to many a heavy burden, grievous to be borne, though it is possible that those who were skilled in all the niceties of the law might find many convenient ways of avoiding troublesome restrictions.

Against this complicated system we have to set the one positive utterance of Christ. 'The Sabbath was made for man'. Even this is called forth by Pharisaic excess and is rather a protest against the Pharisaic Sabbath than a conscious and intentional statement of positive views. Elsewhere the Sabbath has no place in the teachings of Christ, except in so far as He rejects the Sabbath of the Pharisees. Nothing is said about it in the Sermon on the Mount and no parable illustrates its value. So too the Pharisees understood Him. Dispensations from the obligation of the Sabbath in particular cases, difference of opinion on special points might be allowed to a prophet or rabbi and might not invalidate his claim to orthodoxy or to authority. But

---

[1] Taanith IV. 3.   [2] S. Luke xiv. 1—6.

Christ's teaching was far more general, far more revolutionary. Here as elsewhere Christ sought to substitute the spirit for the letter and to do so was to strike at the roots of the Pharisaic system[1].

[1] What is said here is only intended to refer to the Pharisaic Sabbath. It would be foreign to this essay to discuss the relation of the teaching of Christ to the observance of the first day of the week.

CHAPTER VI.

THE STATUS OF WOMEN.

THE bulk of the Mishna, as for instance the treatise on the Sabbath, applies equally to both sexes, and where this is not the case, the same treatise will deal with both. But besides this, one of the six great divisions of the Mishna, containing seven treatises, is devoted specially to the position of women and its title is 'On Women[1]'. One treatise is on the obligation of a brother to marry his deceased brother's widow, another on betrothals, another on marriage settlements, and another on bills of divorce.

The Mishna deliberately and constantly places women on a lower level than men both legally and socially.

Women on lower level.

'Women, slaves and children, are exempt from reciting the Shema, and also from the phylacteries[2]'. 'Women, slaves and children, are exempted from the obligation of living in booths during the Feast of Tabernacles[3]'. It was the custom for the appearance of the new moon, and especially of the new moon which began the new year, to be proved by witnesses. Certain persons were not qualified to

---

[1] Cf. Taylor, *Sayings of the Jewish Fathers*, p. 29, note 12.
[2] Berachoth III. 3.   [3] Succah II. 8.

act as witnesses. 'Gamblers, usurers, pigeon breeders, traders in the produce of the Sabbatical year, and slaves. This is the rule—all evidence that cannot be received from a woman cannot be received from any of these[1]. Again, 'All are bound to appear in the temple, except the deaf, an idiot, a child and an eunuch, and women, and slaves who have not been set free, and the lame and the blind, and the sick and the aged, and the man who cannot go afoot[2]'.

Again, 'The observance of all affirmative precepts of the law, the performance of which is limited to a certain time, is incumbent on males, and not on females[3]'.

It is possibly because women are relieved from some of the precepts of the law, that it is considered doubtful whether they need be instructed in the Scriptures. We certainly read that 'a man should teach his daughter the Scriptures, lest perchance she be compelled to drink the bitter waters of jealousy, in which case the fact that she has studied the Scriptures will defer their harmful effect[4]'. However upon this text the commentators gravely discuss the question whether women should be instructed in the Scriptures[5].

In other matters the rights of the woman are inferior to those of the man. A man may devote his son as a Nazirite, may sell or betroth his daughter; a woman has none of these rights. On the other hand, a woman is in certain cases treated more leniently than a man; she may not be hung, nor may she be sold on account of theft, whereas a man may suffer either of these punishments[6].

[1] Rosh Hashanah I. 8.　　[2] Chagiga I. 1.
[3] Kedushin I. 7.
[4] Cf. Num. v. 11—31. It is assumed that she is guilty.
[5] Sotah III. 4.　　[6] Sotah III. 8.

In all these cases the woman is treated as inferior to the man, and while limited in privileges is also relieved from responsibility.

The introductory section of the treatise on Betrothals treats of women as property in much the same way as it treats of slaves and cattle. A wife is acquired in three ways, two of which are by money and by contract[1]. A Hebrew slave is acquired by money or by contract[2]; a Canaanite slave by money or by contract[3]; immoveable property is acquired by money, moveable property by being removed by the purchaser[4]. Large cattle are acquired by delivery of the animal from the seller to the buyer[5]. All this, it must be remembered, is the introduction to the subject of betrothals, a sort of general treatment of the whole subject of acquiring property before proceeding to the special case of women. This particular species of property seems sometimes to have been treated carelessly. 'When a father says, "I have betrothed my daughter, but do not remember to whom", and a man comes and says, "You betrothed her to me", that man is to be believed[6]'.

<small>Women as property.</small>

On the other hand, a woman is usually spoken of as betrothing herself and not as being betrothed[7] by her father, except in the case of minors, and then provision is made for the repudiation of the betrothal by the woman if she does not approve of it[8].

The legal position of women is summed up thus: 'A woman is always under the authority of her father until she is placed under the authority of her husband[9]'.

---

[1] Kedushin I. 1.   [2] Kedushin I. 2.   [3] Kedushin I. 3.
[4] Kedushin I. 5.   [5] Kedushin I. 4.   [6] Kedushin III. 7.
[7] Kedushin II. 1. [8] Yebamoth XIII. 1, 2.   [9] Ketuboth IV. 3.

The betrothal was an introductory step to this transfer of authority, was formally entered into by both parties, and was important in point of law. The man and woman are spoken of as husband and wife and a bill of divorce was necessary to annul the contract[1]. Any breach of the contract is virtually a breach of a marriage vow.

Hence, when Mary was betrothed to Joseph and was suspected by him of infidelity, he proposed to put her away by a writing of divorce.

Married women's property. A married woman had considerable rights of property. Her Ketubah or marriage settlement is strictly guarded; anything she inherits becomes her property, likewise a share of damages awarded her for insult or injury[2]; but the usufruct of all such property is given to the husband[3]. In return the husband must maintain his wife, must ransom her from captivity and must provide for her interment. He inherits her property at her decease, and a widow must be maintained out of her late husband's property but her Ketubah goes to her heirs[4]. In case she is divorced, without sufficient cause, she takes her property with her.

Household duties. The Mishna is also very explicit about a woman's household duties: 'These are the kinds of work which a woman is bound to do for her husband. She must grind corn and bake and wash and cook and suckle his child and make his bed and work in wool. If she brought him one bondwoman, she needs not to grind, bake or wash; if she brought two, she need not cook nor suckle her child; if she brought three, she need not cook nor work in wool; if she brought four, she may sit in her easy chair. R. Eleazar saith, Even

[1] Kedushin IV. 9.
[2] Ketuboth VI. 1.
[3] Ketuboth VIII.
[4] Ketuboth XI.

though she has brought him a hundred bondwomen, he can compel her to work in wool, as idleness leads to unchastity. R. Simon ben Gamaliel saith, in like manner, Should a man by vow interdict his wife from doing any kind of work, he is bound to divorce her and to pay her the amount of her Ketubah, because idleness may lead to mental aberration[1]'.

Polygamy is taken for granted in the Mishna, a man may betroth himself to five women at once[2]. The various complications arising out of a multiplicity of wives are fully discussed. It is, however, supposed from the Gospels and other writings of the period that the custom of polygamy was dying out and the regulations of the Mishna may be rather a formal completing of the theory of the ancient law than intended for practical use at the time. It should, however, be remembered that the Herods did not confine themselves to one wife at a time. The discord in families to which polygamy might lead may be illustrated by the following provision; 'Everyone is deemed a trustworthy witness to testify to a woman concerning her husband's decease, except her mother-in-law, the daughter of the latter, her own rival (i.e. her husband's other wife), her sister-in-law or her husband's daughter (by another wife)[3]'. To which de Sola and Raphall append the following note, 'Because these females are suspected of bearing her ill-will and may wish to bring her to shame' (by giving her false information, which may lead her to marry a second husband while her first is alive).

Divorce, as is well known, was easy and frequent. Herodias had divorced her husband Philip to marry Herod

Polygamy.

Divorce.

[1] Ketuboth v. 7.   [2] Kedushin ii. 7.
[3] Yebamoth xv. 4.

Antipas. The woman of Samaria had probably been separated from her five husbands by divorce. Naturally there was much controversy as to what constituted valid grounds for divorce. Christ gives His decision on this question in two passages. The first is in the Sermon on the Mount[1]. 'It was said also, Whosoever shall put away his wife, let him give her a writing of divorcement: but I say unto you, that every one that putteth away his wife, saving for the cause of fornication, maketh her an adulteress: and whosoever shall marry her when she is put away committeth adultery'.

The second utterance of Christ on this subject was on His last journey to Jerusalem[2]. The Pharisees came tempting Him and saying, 'Is it lawful for a man to put away his wife for every cause? And He answered and said, Have ye not read, that He which made them from the beginning made them male and female, and said, For this cause shall a man leave his father and mother, and shall cleave to his wife, and the twain shall become one flesh. What therefore God hath joined together, let not man put asunder. They say unto Him, Why then did Moses command to give a bill of divorcement and to put her away? He said unto them, Moses for your hardness of heart suffered you to put away your wives; but from the beginning it hath not been so. And I say unto you, Whosoever shall put away his wife, except for fornication, and shall marry another, committeth adultery: and he that marrieth her when she is put away committeth adultery'. Perhaps one of the striking proofs of the extent to which loose views on marriage were adopted

---

[1] S. Matt. v. 31. Cf. S. Luke xvi. 18, the only reference to the subject in that Gospel.
[2] S. Matt. xix. 3—12; cf. S. Mark x. 2—12.

is to be found in the comment of the disciples, 'If the case of the man is so with his wife, it is not expedient to marry', and the answer of Christ, 'All men cannot receive this saying, but they to whom it is given'. Now the views of the Mishna on this subject are far more in harmony with the practice of certain American states than with the teaching of Christ. The re-marriage of divorced wives and husbands, as in the case of Herodias and the Samaritan woman, is referred to as a matter of course[1] and no attempt is made to limit the practice.

The grounds for divorce which the Mishna recognises as valid are sufficiently numerous to justify one in saying that according to the Rabbis divorce was allowable for any and every cause.

[2] 'The following women are divorced and do not receive their Ketubah:—She who violates the law of Moses or the traditions of the Jews. What constitutes a violation of the law of Moses? If she causes him to eat food that has not paid tithe;...if she vows and does not keep her vow. What constitutes a violation of the traditions of the Jews? If she goes out with her hair loose; if she spins in the streets; if she converses[3] with any man. Abba Saul saith, If she curses his children in his presence. Rabbi Tarphon saith, If she is a noisy woman. What is meant by a noisy woman? One who speaks in her own house so that the neighbours can hear'.

'Beth Shammai[4] say: No man may divorce his wife,

[1] Gittin IV. 8, VIII. 5, 8 and passim.
[2] Ketubah VII. 6.
[3] RR. de Sola and Raphall interpret this as meaning 'flirts'.
[4] The members of the school founded by Shammai, so Beth Hillel of that founded by Hillel.

unless he found in her scandalous behaviour, for it is said[1]: Because he found in her some scandalous behaviour; but Beth Hillel say: Even if she spoiled his food. R. Akiba saith: Even if he found one handsomer than her, for it is said[1]: If it happen that she found no favour in his eyes'.

It also appears that divorce might be a matter of arrangement or the subject of a bargain between man and wife, for we read: 'If he (the husband) says: Here is your bill of divorce on condition that you give me 200 zooz; she is divorced from the moment she accepts the bill of divorce and is bound to pay the stipulated amount[2]'.

RR. de Sola and Raphall however, in their note on the decisions of Beth Shammai and Beth Hillel, state that R. Akiba's decision is not accepted, and that neither Beth Hillel nor R. Akiba would intend to apply their decision to practical life. They also state that the Talmud always discourages divorce and only permits it under peculiar circumstances and for a legal object. They quote the concluding words of the Gemara on the treatise Gittin. R. Eleazar saith, "Even the altar drops tears when a man divorces the wife and companion of his youth, for thus[3] is it written, 'And this have ye done again covering the altar of the Lord with tears, with weeping, and with crying out... Yet ye say, Wherefore? Because the Lord hath been witness between thee and the wife of thy youth, against whom thou hast dealt treacherously, although she is thy companion and the wife of thy covenant".

It is possible that these teachers did not intend their extreme doctrines to be acted upon, but it is pretty certain

---

[1] Deut. xxiv.   [2] Gittin vii. 5.
[3] Mal. ii. 13, 14.

that these doctrines would serve as excuses for evil-disposed persons, and it is clear from the Gospel narratives and other authorities that this was the case. Take for instance the following statement of Josephus in his autobiography[1], 'And at this time I divorced my wife, the mother of three children, because I was not pleased with her manners'. A few lines further down he tells us that he married again. RR. de Sola and Raphall themselves tell us that it is mentioned in the treatise Baba Kama, that the priests were often in the habit of divorcing their wives in sudden fits of passion, and repented soon after; when, as priests, it was unlawful for them to take them back, after having been once divorced. To meet this difficulty a special form of bill of divorce was devised which could not become valid till after some delay. It was hoped that this delay might give time for the priests to become calm that they and their wives might be reconciled. Here the behaviour of the priests seems to indicate that they at any rate carried out practically what R. Akiba and Beth Hillel taught.

Much has been made of a story quoted in Lightfoot[2] of a certain Rabbi Nachman, who on arriving at a village to spend the night there, used to send round a herald for a wife for the time of his stay. Surely the prosaic literalness of Western criticism goes too far when it supposes that this was intended for history. It is probably one of the grim pleasantries with which the Rabbis delight to bewilder and confound their readers. Amidst all this laxity as to divorce it is curious to find extreme strictness on other points; it seems to be implied[3] that if a man has been

---

[1] § 76. [2] *Hor. Hebr.* Matt. xix. 3. [3] Kedushin III. 10.

betrothed to a woman and the betrothal has not been completed by marriage, the man is not allowed to marry any of the woman's relatives.

The Levirate Law.   If a woman were left a widow without children, the law of Moses directed that her husband's brother should marry her. Copious directions intended to exhaust all possible cases are given in the treatise on this subject. One case may remind us of the story by which the Sadducees tried to puzzle Christ, the story in which a woman was married to seven brothers one after the other. The case is as follows:

'When a man, who had received information of his wife's death, married her sister from the father's side only, and upon receipt of intelligence of the death of this latter, marries her maternal sister; and on the news of the decease of the last mentioned, marries her sister from the father's side; and, finally, on the reported death of this latter, marries her maternal sister. It turns out that the information has in each case been incorrect and all the five women are alive[1]'. The passage goes on to explain, which are his wives and which of them his brother would be bound to marry in case of his death.

From all that has been quoted on this subject it will be gathered that the Jews of this period were seriously tainted with the immorality that was eating away the vigour of the Roman Empire. Indeed Roman and Greek writers tell us that the Jews were notorious as taking a leading part in the infamous trade in vice. And the Mishna itself tells us that because of the increase of murderers the ceremony of the Heifer for the expiation of uncertain murder was aban-

[1] Yebamoth x. 5.

doned, and because of the increase of adultery the ceremony of the waters of jealousy was abandoned[1]. The latter fact throws some light on the feigned zeal for morality on the part of the Pharisees in the case of the woman taken in adultery.

A less disagreeable question in connection with the status of women is that of the extent of freedom of social intercourse allowed to them. It is evident from the Gospels that we cannot ascribe to Jewish women that seclusion of the harem, that jealous life-long imprisonment, which is said to be the lot in the present day of Eastern women of the middle and higher classes. They appear in public, are present at feasts at any rate to serve the guests, and some even follow Christ from place to place with the other disciples. Probably the Pharisees disapproved of this. Even the command that the women should keep silence in the churches implies considerable liberty. *Freedom of Social Intercourse.*

Nor are there in the Mishna traces of seclusion. It is true that it is matter for grave suspicion if a woman is seen conversing with a strange man in the street[2]. A woman is not to keep a school, for fear of scandal arising through the visits of the parents of the scholars[3]. There are also cautions against talking too much with women, which may help us to understand the astonishment of the disciples at finding Christ talking to a woman[4]. José ben Jochanan says, 'Prolong not converse with a woman', and a gloss adds, 'His own wife is meant, much less a neighbour's[5]'. All these precautions tend to shew that women had opportunities

---

[1] Sotah ix. 9. [2] Ketuboth i. 8.
[3] Kedushin iv. 13. [4] S. John iv. 27.
[5] Pirke Aboth i. 5, 6.

of meeting with men, a certain freedom of social intercourse.

It is also likely that in general the actual position of women was better than the legal provisions on the subject might lead us to suppose.

CHAPTER VII.

ETHICS AND DOCTRINE.

THE Mishna is too much occupied in attempting to apply the Law and the Tradition to all the possible contingencies of daily life to have much time to spare for general principle. At least the kind of general principle worked out in the Mishna is, as before stated, fairly illustrated by 'Thou shalt not sow thy field with mingled seed', 'Thou shalt not carry burdens on the Sabbath'. Out of the abundance of the heart the mouth speaketh, and if the Pharisees left undone the weightier matters of the law, judgment, and mercy, and faith; the Mishna says very little about them[1]. What little there is said is mainly collected in one treatise out of the sixty, 'Pirke Aboth' or 'Aboth', 'Fathers', or as it is sometimes called in English, 'Sayings of the Fathers'.

The treatise Aboth is unique in the Mishna, here and Aboth. elsewhere the manifold elaboration of ritual or moral minutiæ is broken by a doctrinal or ethical saying, but the treatise Aboth stands alone in being made up of such. The gather-

[1] It is true that the Hagadic writings deal more with spiritual matters, but the pre-eminent position assigned to the Mishna justifies what is said in the text.

ing together of these into one treatise reminds one of the grouping of Christ's sayings in the Sermon on the Mount, and one might say that the Aboth is to the Mishna as the Sermon on the Mount is to the Gospel, or as the Epistles to the Seven Churches are to the Apocalypse, or as the twenty-sixth chapter of Leviticus is to the book of Leviticus; only the difference between Aboth and the rest of the Mishna is much more striking than in the other cases.

This treatise being for all other than antiquarian purposes by far the most profitable and interesting part of the Mishna is often published alone, it is the storehouse from which many writers draw their gems of Talmudic wisdom, but it is not to be supposed that Aboth or any set of quotations from it is a fair specimen of the Mishna.

It consists chiefly of a series of short paragraphs, each containing from one to half-a-dozen sayings, attributed to some one of the successive teachers who in their turn received and transmitted the tradition from Ezra to Rabbi Judah himself. For instance, the Gamaliel of the Acts is represented by the following saying, 'Rabban Gamaliel said, Make to thyself a master, and be quit of doubt; and tithe not much by conjecture'.

Thus in a few pages we have the selected wisdom of centuries of orthodox Jewish thought.

Possibly in each case the sayings preserved were favourite truths of the Rabbis to whom they are ascribed. The Rabbis often repeated them till their hearers remembered them and learnt to associate them with those particular teachers. Thus the Seven Sages of Greece are remembered by a saying apiece. Had Jesus of Nazareth been an orthodox Rabbi, He might have been represented by some such sayings as these: 'He that hath ears to hear, let him hear¹', 'Many that are first shall be last²', 'Many are called but few are chosen'.³

It is true that if we remember the main characteristics of the Mishna, which are those of a law-book, these sayings seem out of place. But their position here serves to illustrate the determined recognition on the part of the Jews of the union of social and legal with ethical and religious teaching. This is also illustrated in something the same way by the contents of the Pentateuch and the prophecies of Ezekiel; but in neither of the latter are primary truths thrust into the background that minor truths may be painfully worked out and often distorted by being considered apart from their relations to the greater truths on which they rest.

It will follow from the fragmentary character of this teaching that there is no regular development, no scientific statement of principles or doctrines. We may however quote to shew how Jewish teachers summarized in proverbial statements the truths which underlay the system of the Mishna. As a rule the truths are better than the system.

i. *The Law.* As we might naturally expect we find a great deal on the value of the Law or of 'instruction⁴', the duty of studying it, and the fruitful results thereof.

According to Simon the Just the world rests on three things; the Torah, the Temple service, and the bestowal of kindnesses⁵. Simeon ben Gamaliel however says, the

---

¹ Matt. xi. 15, xiii. 9, 43; Mark iv. 9, 23, vii. 16, viii. 18; Luke viii. 8; xiv. 35.
² Matt. xix. 30, xx. 16 and parallels.   ³ Matt. xx. 16, xxii. 14.
⁴ Cf. Taylor, *Sayings of the Jewish Fathers*, p. 119.   ⁵ I. 2.

world stands on three things; judgment, truth, and peace[1]. Man is created for Torah[2], and Torah is one of the five possessions of God[3]. There are three crowns, the crown of Torah, the crown of Priesthood, and the crown of Royalty; but the crown of a good name is above them[4]. Elsewhere it is said that the Torah is greater than the priesthood and the kingdom[5].

If three eat at one table, and have not said over it words of Torah, they are as if they had eaten the sacrifices of the dead[6]. Where there is no Torah there is no culture[7].

If there is much Torah, there is much reward[8], for Torah gives life in this world and in the world to come[9]. The observance of it brings honour[10] and wealth, if a man neglects it he comes to poverty[11]. He who takes upon him the yoke of Torah is relieved from the yoke of royalty and worldly care[12]. The Shekinah or Divine Presence is with those who occupy themselves about Torah[13].

'He that profanes things sacred, and contemns the festivals, and annuls the covenant of Abraham our father, and acts barefacedly against the Torah, even though he be a doer of good works, has no portion in the world to come[14]', but on the other hand it is said, 'All Torah without work must fail and occasion iniquity'. Torah almost seems with the Rabbis to occupy the place of faith with S. Paul and S. James, for with them without faith works are dead, and without works faith is dead.

[1] I. 19. The quotations in this chapter are mostly from the section Aboth.
[2] II. 9. Cf. Nedarim III. 11, where it is said the world was created on account of circumcision. In Christian writers the world is said to be created on account of the Church.
[3] VI. 10. [4] IV. 19. [5] VI. 6. [6] III. 5.
[7] III. 26. [8] I. 19. [9] VI. 7. [10] IV. 10.
[11] IV. 13. [12] III. 8. [13] III. 1. [14] III. 17, II. 2.

'Whosoever is busied in Torah for its own sake merits many things; and not only so, but he is worth the whole world: he is called friend, beloved: loves God, loves mankind: pleases God, pleases mankind. And it clothes him with meekness and fear, and fits him to become righteous, pious, upright and faithful: and removes him from sin, and brings him towards the side of merit...And he becomes modest and long-suffering and forgiving of insult[1]'. So that Torah is like that 'love' in the great thirteenth of First Corinthians, love which suffereth long and is not puffed up; and reminds one also of 'faith' in the eleventh chapter of the Hebrews; so that one feels that the whole matter is fitly summed up by Ben Bag Bag, when he says of Torah, 'Turn it and again turn it; for the all is therein and thy all is therein; and swerve not therefrom for thou canst have no greater excellency than this[2]'.

ii. *Good Works.* Some reference has already been made to this subject in speaking of the Torah.

Good works.

Submission to God is inculcated, but from somewhat selfish motives.

'Do His will as if it were thy will, that He may do thy will, as if it were His will. Annul thy will before His will, that He may annul the will of others before thy will[3]'; but Antigonus of Socho, the founder of the Sadducees, says, 'Be not as slaves that minister to the lord with a view to receive recompense[4]'.

Much also is said in praise of kindliness and beneficence towards men. The good way that a man should cleave to is a good heart, the evil way an evil heart[5]. Hillel said, 'Be

[1] vi. 1.   [2] v. 32.   [3] ii. 4.   [4] i. 3.   [5] ii. 12, 13.

of the disciples of Aaron, loving peace and pursuing peace; loving mankind and bringing them near to the Torah[1]".

The bestowal of kindnesses is one of the three things on which the world rests[2]. It is also said, 'Let the needy be thy household[3]', Repentance and good works are a shield against punishment[4]. So in case of a fast an aged man is to say, Brethren it is not said for the men of Nineveh, 'And God saw their sackcloth and their fasting' but 'God saw their works, that they returned from their evil way', and it is said, 'Rend your hearts and not your garments, and turn unto the Lord your God[5]'.

The necessity of supporting mere knowledge of truth by practical holiness is enforced thus:

'Whosoever wisdom is in excess of his works, to what is he like? To a tree whose branches are abundant, and its roots scanty; and the wind comes, and uproots it and overturns it. And whosesoever works are in excess of his wisdom, to what is he like? To a tree whose branches are scanty, and its roots abundant; though all the winds come upon it, they stir it not from its place[6]'.

It is interesting to find among all this praise of the Torah and of its teachers the following tribute to a virtue often not sufficiently appreciated. It almost seems as if the teachers sometimes wearied their scholars. Simeon son of Gamaliel said, "All my days I have grown up amongst the wise, and have not found aught good for a man but silence; not learning but doing is the groundwork; and whoso multiplies words occasions sin[7]". Compare with this the saying of Rabbi Akiba, "A fence to wisdom is silence[8]".

[1] I. 13. [2] I. 2. [3] I. 5. [4] IV. 15. [5] Taanith II.1.
[6] III. 27; cf. S. Matt. vii. 24. [7] I. 18. [8] III. 20.

ETHICS AND DOCTRINE. 85

Sincerity and the Doctrine of Intention.

From what has been said about Good Works it will be Sincerity. evident that the Mishna is not wanting in exhortations to practical morality; the sincerity of profession is to be guaranteed by performance. There are also sayings which lay stress on the necessity of spiritual earnestness as well as of accurate ceremonial. "Men are not to stand up to pray except with profound humility. The pious men of ancient days used to pause a full hour before they began to pray, in order to direct their minds to the Deity[1]". A similar spirit is manifested in the following comment on Exod. xvii. 11, "When Moses held up his hand then Israel prevailed, &c." "Could the hands of Moses animate the contest, or cause it to cease? But it was thus: whilst Israel looked to heaven for aid, and subjected their will to their heavenly Father, they prevailed, but when they ceased to do so, they failed". Again on Num. xxi. 8, "Make thee a fiery serpent, and set it on a pole, and every one that is bitten, when he looketh upon it shall live". "Could this serpent kill or bring to life? But it was thus: when the Israelites looked to heaven for aid, and subjected their inclination to the will of their heavenly Father, they were cured, but when they did not, they perished[2]". It even seems that a silent intention to pray was valid, even if it found no outward expression. We read, "If one who is reading in the Law when the time comes for praying intends it in his heart? He is free. But if not? He is not free[3]". The meaning of this passage seems to be that if anyone is reading the Law at the time

[1] Berachoth v. 1.   [2] Rosh Hashanah III. 8.
[3] Berachoth II. 1.

86   ETHICS AND DOCTRINE.

when the Shema should be pronounced and, rather than interrupt his reading, silently directs his thoughts to the Shema, he is to be considered as having discharged the obligation of repeating it.

Intention. This care for inward sincerity may if pressed become mechanical. In the Mishna we find the Doctrine of Intention fairly anticipated[1]. In order that a ceremony performed by a private individual for his own benefit may be effectual thereunto, every stage of the ceremony must have been gone through with the intention that it should be a part of that particular ceremony. If a man washes himself with the intention of eating ordinary food this washing does not purify him for eating of tithes[1]. The Passover lamb must be slaughtered with the intention that it shall be for the Passover and with the intention that it shall be for a definite company[2], otherwise it is unlawful.

According to the Council of Trent the failure of a right intention in the officiating priest destroys the efficacy of the sacraments. A similar result seems to follow from the rules of the Mishna as to the necessity of a right intention on the part of the High Priest in discharging his duties. This necessity is specially insisted on in the case of the Passover[3] and the ceremony of the Red Heifer[4].

In laying stress on a right intention in the case of certain actions an inevitable danger is incurred. In judging of his intentions a man is judge, jury, counsel, witnesses and a party to the suit all in one and must often be tempted to persuade himself that his intentions were such as they

[1] Chagiga II. 6.   [2] Pesachim VI. 6.
[3] Pesachim V. 2.
[4] Parah IV. 1, XII. 2, 3; cf. Barclay's note in loco.

should have been. He will often succumb to the temptation. In addition to such cases as the above there are others in which the inducement to hypocrisy would be peculiarly strong. Work done on the Sabbath unintentionally may be made use of. Are there not many odd pieces of work that a man might do almost by accident and afterwards persuade himself that it was quite by accident?

iii. *The Divine Sovereignty.* According to Josephus[1] the Pharisees taught that all things happened by divine decree, but yet they did not deny the free will of man. Rabbi Akiba states the same truth thus: 'Everything is foreseen; and freewill is given. And the world is judged by grace; and everything is according to work[2]'. Again S. Paul, the pupil of Gamaliel, applies the same apparent paradox to practical life thus: 'Work out your own salvation with fear and trembling, for it is God that worketh in you both to will and to do of His good pleasure.'

Divine Sovereignty.

There are a few practical remarks which may perhaps be traced to a belief in the Divine Sovereignty and in these the Rabbis are happier than is their wont. Man is to bless God for evil as well as for good[3].

It is also said, and the saying is virtually an assertion of the all-controlling wisdom of God, 'Despise not any man, and carp not at anything; for thou wilt find that there is not a man that has not his hour, and not a thing that has not its place[4]'. We are also reminded that our lives are part of a great plan and that our share in it is assigned

[1] *Antt.* XVIII. i. 3; *B. J.* II. viii. 14. [2] III. 24.
[3] Berachoth IX. 5. The subsequent explanation of this saying is rather unfortunate.
[4] IV. 6.

88   ETHICS AND DOCTRINE.

to us by God, and that it is beyond us to say what our work shall be, to what extent we shall be allowed to complete it, or when we may lay it aside; for it is said, 'It is not for thee to finish the work, nor art thou free to desist therefrom[1]'. A sterner aspect of the same truth is given in the following saying, 'Let not thine imagination assure thee that the grave is an asylum; for without thine own consent thou wast framed, and without thine own consent thou livest, and without thine own consent thou diest, and without thine own consent thou art about to give account and reckoning before the King of the kings of kings, the Holy One, blessed is He[2]'.

Future life.

iv. *The Future Life.* The Acts of the Apostles says of the Pharisees that they believed in the resurrection, in angels and spirits, while the Sadducees believed in none of those things[3]. Josephus also tells us that the Pharisees believed in a future life[4], and in one place speaks of the soul as passing into another body[5]; which might seem to imply the transmigration of the soul. But as this doctrine is not elsewhere ascribed to the Pharisees, it is possible that it may be a somewhat awkward equivalent of our phrase 'resurrection of the body'.

In S. John[6] the Jews, that is to say, the Pharisees, for all really orthodox Jews were Pharisees, are spoken of as thinking to find 'eternal life' in their Scriptures.

The doctrine of the future life is clearly laid down in the Mishna, the phrases 'the world to come' and the 'life to

[1] II. 19.   [2] IV. 32.   [3] Acts xxiii. 8.
[4] *Antt.* XVIII. i. 3.   [5] *B. J.* II. viii. 14.
[6] S. John v. 39.

ETHICS AND DOCTRINE.   89

come' occur frequently, sometimes in opposition to 'the world[1]'. The 'Garden of Eden' is spoken of as the reward of the righteous[2]. In one passage[3] the opposite doctrine is distinctly controverted. It is said, "All the seals of the blessings in the sanctuary used to say, 'from the עולם'. But since the Epicureans perversely taught there is but one עולם, it was directed that men should say, 'from עולם to עולם'".

The word עולם is represented in Greek by αἰών. Its original meaning is 'age' and then 'world', then the phrase 'from the age' came to mean eternity. The Epicureans, that is to say, heretics, caught up the words 'the age' and used it as a proof that there was only one 'age', one 'world', one state in which men lived, and to meet this trivial and frivolous argument, the formula was changed so as literally to imply the existence of two worlds, a future life as well as a present.

In the face of this it is rather strange to read, 'The death of the wicked is pleasant for them and pleasant for the world; but the death of the righteous is evil for them and evil for the world[4]'.

It almost seems as if the doctrine of the future life was not yet clearly understood, and its consequences were not properly worked out.

The mystical and miraculous are a much more prominent feature of the Gemara than of the Mishna; but still they are sufficiently marked in the latter. In the Gospels we read that Christ at His Baptism, at the Transfiguration and shortly

Mysticism.

[1] II. 8, 19, IV. 3, 24, VI. 7; Sanhedrim x. 1. Cf. Taylor, *Sayings of the Jewish Fathers*, on II. 19; also N. T. passim, ὁ αἰὼν ὁ ἐρχομενος and ὁ μέλλων αἰών, Mark x. 30, &c.
[2] v. 29, 31.   [3] Berachoth IX. 5.   [4] Sanhedrim VIII. 5.

before His Passion¹ was addressed by a voice from heaven. A 'voice from heaven', the 'Bath Kol' or 'daughter of the voice', is frequently referred to by Jewish writers. Thus 'Every day Bath Kol goes forth from Mount Horeb, and makes proclamation and says, Woe to the creatures for contempt of Torah²'.

According to the Mishna the temple services were the occasion of a numerous set of regular miracles. On the Day of Atonement a scarlet thread twisted on the door of the Sanctuary turned white when the scape-goat arrived in the wilderness³.

'Ten miracles were wrought in the sanctuary⁴'. Among these were the following: 'The holy meat never stank...a fly was not seen in the slaughterhouse; and a defect was not found in the sheaf; nor in the two loaves; nor in the shewbread'.

A special significance is also attached to certain seasons: 'The world is judged at four periods; at the passover, for the growth of corn; at pentecost, for the fruit of trees; at new year's day, when all human beings pass before Him like lambs, as is said, "He fashioneth their hearts alike; He considereth all their works"; and at the feast of tabernacles, judgment is given for the rains⁵'.

It may however be doubted whether in these accounts of miracles we ought to see anything more than a highly figurative statement of certain moral and spiritual truths.

We also find traces of the ordinary belief in omens and charms. If a man pray, and make a mistake, it is a bad sign for him. If he be a representative of a congregation, it

---

¹ S. John xii. 28.   ² vi. 2.   ³ Yoma vi. 8.
⁴ v. 8.   ⁵ Rosh Hashanah i. 2.

is a bad sign for those whom he represents, for a man's representative is like himself. They say of R. Hanina, son of Dosa, that when he prayed for the sick, he used to say, "this one will live", or "this one will die." They said to him, "how do you know?" He said to them, "if my prayer be fluent in my mouth, I know that he is accepted; but if not, I know that he is lost[1]".

Among the things which may be carried on the Sabbath are included according to some, 'an egg of a locust, and a tooth of a fox, and a nail of one crucified, as medicine[2]'. According to others it is forbidden to carry such things at all 'because of the ways of the Amorites', i.e. because such practices savoured of heathen magic.

The fifth chapter of the Pirke Aboth exemplifies the tendency to attach special importance to certain numbers. Omitting two or three short paragraphs, the chapter is arranged thus; nine sets of ten, ten sayings by which the world was created, ten generations from Adam to Noah, &c.; three sets of seven; seven sets of four, mostly sets of four characters; two sets of three.

[1] Berachoth v. 5. [2] Sabbath vi. 10.

CHAPTER VIII.

Vows. The Poor.

Vows. THE custom of making vows does not occupy any prominent place in the Gospels. John the Baptist indeed is a Nazirite, and Christ in His denunciation of the Pharisees includes among their other sins the fact that they say, 'If a man shall say to his father or his mother, That wherewith thou mightest have been profited by me is Corban, that is to say, Given to God' and 'no longer suffer him to do aught for his father or his mother; making void the word of God by their traditions[1]'. There is a treatise in the Mishna on the Nazirite vow and also one on vows in general. 'Corban' is one of a group of words of similar meaning used in the Mishna in the forms of vows. In one passage an opinion is given as to the relative validity in such forms of 'Corban', 'as Corban', 'the Corban', 'for Corban' respectively, and some doubt seems to exist as to the validity of the last phrase[1].

The phrases too 'wherein I might be profited by you', 'wherein you might be profited by me', are among the regular forms of vows[2]. We meet with two classes of vows

[1] Nedarim I. 4. [2] Nedarim VIII. 7.

of this kind, vows by which a man binds himself either not to receive any advantage from some one or not to do anything that will be of advantage to the other party. It seems that such vows were so frequent, especially in Galilee, as to interfere with social life and cause serious inconvenience. With a view to obviating this difficulty synagogues and other public buildings are reckoned as belonging to the prince that they may not be subject to such vows and so may be freely used[1].

The treatise on vows discusses with the usual minuteness the particular forms of vows that are valid and in what particular cases, also with what degree of rigour the words of a vow are to be interpreted. For instance, if a man has vowed not to eat beans, may he eat French beans or is he only debarred from broad beans[2]. As oaths and vows cannot easily be distinguished both are virtually discussed in the treatise 'Vows'. Christ in speaking of oaths says, 'Swear not at all; neither by heaven, for it is the throne of God; nor by the earth, for it is the footstool of His feet; nor by Jerusalem, for it is the city of the great King[3]'. Now among the valid forms of oath in the Mishna are the altar, the temple, and Jerusalem, only Rabbi Judah says that if any man swears by Jerusalem it is as if he said nothing[4].

With this we have to compare Matt. xxiii. 16—22, 'Woe unto you, ye blind guides, which say, Whosoever shall swear by the temple, it is nothing; but whosoever shall swear by the gold of the temple, he is a debtor...Whosoever shall swear by the altar, it is nothing; but whosoever shall swear by the gift that is upon it, he is a debtor. Ye blind: for

[1] Nedarim v. 5. [2] This is only an imaginary example.
[3] Matt. v. 35. [4] Nedarim I. 3.

whether is greater, the gift, or the altar that sanctifieth the gift?' Between the Gospel and the Mishna as it now stands there is a discrepancy, but the saying of Rabbi Judah suggests the existence of a popular practice in accordance with the words of the Gospel, but possibly disallowed in later times. The saying 'the altar sanctifieth what belongs to it (lit. is worthy of it)', occurs in another connection in the Mishna[1].

The provisions for absolving men from inconvenient vows are as minute and elaborate as the discussion of the forms and scope of vows. Four classes of vows need not be observed, (i) Vows of persuasion, (ii) Hyperbolical Vows, (iii) Vows as to which a mistake is made, (iv) Vows which cannot be performed owing to adverse circumstances. Vows of persuasion are illustrated by the oaths made use of in negotiating a bargain. The seller swears he will not take less than two shekels, the buyer swears he will not give more than one. These incompatible vows are not allowed to put an end to the negotiation, but may both be disregarded and the buyer and seller may agree on an intermediate price. Hyperbolical vows are vows in which the condition is impossible in the nature of things, e.g. I will do so and so if I see a serpent in the shape of a triangle. Mistaken vows are those in which a man makes or breaks a vow under a false impression, vows 'if I have eaten', forgetting that he has eaten, or 'if I shall eat', and afterwards forgets his vow and eats. Vows annulled by circumstances are those in which the performance of a vow is not known to be impossible when the vow is made, but is afterwards found to be so, as for instance when a man vows to take a journey and after-

[1] Zebachim IX. 1.

wards finds that the floods are out and he cannot go[1]. There are other curious regulations for the benefit of those who made hasty vows or oaths. If a vow was made in the faith that the Sages could absolve the man, he was to be absolved[2]; and if a man made a vow that if a man were made scribe he would do so and so; making the vow in the belief that the man was not a scribe, and then found out that he was a scribe, the vow was not valid. If the casuistry of the Mishna is not exactly the same as that attributed to the Pharisees by Christ it is very similar in character.

One of the leading features of the Old Testament is its care for the needs of the poor. The legislation of the Old Testament secures them many rights and provides for their relief when in distress. The crime which the prophets denounce most frequently and emphatically is the oppression of the poor. *The Poor: Attitude of Old Testament.*

It is unnecessary to point out that Christ in this matter fully endorses the teaching of the Old Testament. The strongest proof of this is that He Himself was a working man and chose His friends and disciples from the same class. We read 'Blessed are the poor,' and it is hard for 'a rich man to enter into the kingdom of heaven'. His command is, 'Give to him that asketh of thee'. His invitation is given to all who are 'weary and heavy laden'. Doubtless in all these sayings there is a spiritual meaning, but the willingness of Christ to relieve physical suffering warrants us in including in them actual poverty and weariness of toil. *Attitude of Christ.*

The Mishna in its own peculiar way is equally faithful to the teaching of the Old Testament, and the rights granted therein to the poor are carefully maintained. For instance *Attitude of Mishna.*

[1] Nedarim III. 1.   [2] Nazir II. 4.

96   VOWS. THE POOR.

'Corner of a field'.
we read, 'When ye reap the harvest of your land, thou shalt not make clean riddance of the corners of thy field when thou reapest, neither shalt thou gather any gleaning of thy harvest: thou shalt leave them to the poor, and to the stranger: I am the Lord your God¹'.

A treatise² of the Mishna is devoted to the subject of this corner of a field.

Special indulgence.
The difficulties arising out of the uncertainty as to whether food had been tithed have been referred to. Special license as to the use of food in such cases is accorded for the purpose of entertaining a poor man on the Sabbath³.

Labourers and the Sabbatical year.
All debts according to the Pentateuch were to be released in the Sabbatical Year, but labourers' wages are not released⁴.

Casuals.
A poor man lodging for the night or for the Sabbath is to be supplied with meals. But anyone possessing fifty denarii⁵ is not eligible for this relief⁶. Is it possible that He who had not where to lay His head may sometimes have availed Himself of this provision?

Wine at the Passover.
It is also commanded concerning 'the poorest in Israel' that 'they must not withhold from him the four cups of wine, even though he receive the weekly alms⁷'.

Slaves.
The Mishna contains comparatively little as to the position of slaves. They were disqualified from discharging certain legal and ceremonial functions. Gamaliel seems to have had a slave Tabbi to whom he was much attached and who possessed some knowledge of the law⁸.

Denunciation of
The provisions on behalf of the poor are enforced by

¹ Lev. xxiii. 22.   ² Peah.   ³ Demai iv. 4.
⁴ Shebiith x. 1.   ⁵ זוז.   ⁶ Peah viii. 7, 9.
⁷ Peshachim x. 1.   ⁸ Succah ii. 1.

solemn warning, 'At four seasons the pestilence waxes: in the fourth year, in the seventh, in the ending of the seventh; and at the ending of the Feast[1] in every year. In the fourth year, on account of the poor's tithe in the third; in the seventh, on account of the poor's tithe in the sixth; and at the ending of the seventh, on account of the seventh year fruits; and at the ending of the Feast in every year, on account of the largesses of the poor'. wrong to the poor.

In discussing this subject the well-known care of modern Jews for their poor should not be forgotten. Herein they are singularly faithful to the teaching of their traditions. Present condition of Jewish poor.

[1] Tabernacles.

CHAPTER IX.

RELATION OF THE MISHNA AND THE GOSPELS TO THE OLD TESTAMENT.

The Mishna and the Gospel as fulfilling the Old Testament. IT is written in the closing verses of the Book of the Prophet Malachi 'Remember ye the law of Moses my servant, which I commanded unto him in Horeb for all Israel, with the statutes and judgments'. There follows the promise that Elijah shall come before the great and dreadful day of the Lord, and so the book ends. Thus at the end of the Old Testament as arranged in our English Bible, the last of the prophets addresses to Israel as the last word of the prophetic order an exhortation to remember the Law. The Alexandrine school of Jewish thought as represented by the Apocrypha and by Philo was not unmindful of this command; but the Law is remembered most directly and thoroughly in the Gospel of Christ and the Mishna of the Rabbis. Each of these connects directly with the tendency of Jewish thought, as we find it at the close of the Old Testament Canon. So far as either is the result of previous writings or teaching, it is the result of the Old Testament. To the Mishna the Law is all and in all; Christ came to

RELATION OF THE MISHNA TO THE OLD TESTAMENT. 99

fulfil the law giving the assurance, that not one jot or tittle of it should pass away till all should be fulfilled.

The materials for historically connecting either Mishna or Gospel with the Old Testament are scanty, we have no literature which really links the closing books of the Old Testament with the revived Jewish literature of the Gospel or of the Rabbinical schools. Chronologically indeed the Jewish literature of Alexandria[1] fills the gap, but the influence of this literature on either Mishna or Gospel is very slight. Alexandria indeed exercises some influence on the Gospel through the Septuagint, but the Mishna seems to show no traces of such influence. The Mishna gives a list of names connecting Rabbi Judah with Ezra, and assigns one or two sentences to each. It claims moreover to be in the main a reproduction of oral teaching handed down from Moses. So far the connection is complete, but we have little but these sentences to show us when the minute and detailed system of the Mishna arose, to what circumstances it was due and through what forms the oral tradition passed. The claim of the Jews on behalf of the Mishna that it dates back to Moses necessarily involves the neglect or suppression of any evidence that might have thrown light on its actual origin. Obviously the Mishna links itself with parts of the Pentateuch and Ezekiel and the later prophets, also with the Books of Proverbs and Ecclesiastes. It is not unnatural that the legal provisions and proverbial wisdom of the Old Testament should have had their development in later times. However much we may wonder at the extreme form which the development takes in the Mishna, yet even

How do the Mishna and Gospel connect with the Old Testament?

[1] It must be remembered that we are dealing with the Gospels and not with the New Testament as a whole.

here its system is scarcely unique as a specimen either of civil or ecclesiastical law. But the real phenomenon of Jewish thought as illustrated by the Mishna is the failure of the prophetic and spiritual elements of the Old Testament to beget a derivative literature amongst Palestinian Jews. This failure is illustrated and partly explained by the position of authority accorded to the Mishna; for it was the object of the Mishna to deal with the Law. Again the fact should be noticed that what there is of more spiritual teaching in the Hagada is largely grouped round the Mishna. It may perhaps be possible to trace in the later books of the Old Testament the beginning of this tendency to give an undue prominence to legal ordinances.

It cannot be said that either the Alexandrine writings or the Oral Tradition fill the gap in time between the Evangelical teachings of the great prophets and its development in the Gospels. In Stanley's *Jewish Church* the various influences at work on the Jewish character are carefully investigated, but there is little or nothing which indicates any teaching transmitted through Jewish teachers, which coming between the Prophets and the Gospels rises to anything like the elevation of either. It is true that the language and sayings of Christ seem to be influenced by the older Rabbinical teachings, but the essential elements of His teaching, so far as they rest on any original, go back directly to the Old Testament.

The chief element in contemporary Jewish life and thought, which may have supplied impulse, inspiration and enthusiasm for new developments in Jewish literature was the expectation of the immediate advent of the Messiah. The Jewish communities were everywhere seething with excitement and agitated by the wildest hopes. Hence the Old Testament must have had a more living meaning and excited a deeper interest, and those elements of Old Testament teaching which appealed to men's highest hopes and loftiest impulses might be expected to come to the front and to have a dominant influence. This seems to have taken place in at least three ways, according to the differing character of men's highest hopes and impulses. Everyone expected the realization of his ideal. Men of military and patriotic ambition were kindled by the history of Israel's ancient glory and by the seeming promise of empire. Perhaps the rebellion of Barchochabh was the most mature result of the Messianic hope in this direction, the most determined and the most disastrous attempt to realize the ideal of an earthly Messianic kingdom. The men of the schools in their turn applied themselves with renewed vigour to adapt the ancient law to the new condition of things, that the new kingdom might be administered according to the divine will, and Israel in her renewed empire be pure and blameless before her God. But there was no such new kingdom or renewed empire as the Rabbis had anticipated, and their work has come down to us modified by the ruin and failure of their hopes, and this work is embodied in the Mishna. But there were others who sought for more than earthly glory, for more than a perfect system of civil and ceremonial law; there would be men who would be led by the awakening of life and thought to dwell upon the spiritual and moral beauty of the old writings, and to interpret the Messianic hope as a promise that the manifest presence of God, the inspiration of the ancient prophets, should be renewed for them. Christ invited such to find in Himself the realization of their ideal, and the Gospel is the history written by such men of His claims upon their faith and their response to these claims. But making allowance for the different influences that gave rise to the Mishna and the Gospel, it is yet important to remember that it is the same spiritual revelation as contained in Law, Prophets, and Psalms, and as illustrated by Jewish history, that culminated for the Jews in the Mishna and the Talmud, and for us in Christ. Rabbinical teaching and Christianity are two offshoots from the same stock of ancient Judaism and we must not let the vast difference between the two blind us to the fact. To us it may seem that Christianity is the continuation of the main trunk, and modern Judaism a side shoot, feeble and stunted, but both have grown up from the same roots and are nourished by the same spiritual life.

To which section of the Old Testament do the Mishna and the Gospel specially attach themselves?

It has already been pointed out more than once that the Mishna is specially and avowedly connected with the Pentateuch and belongs, with portions of Ezekiel, to those Jewish writings which deal with the Law. The Pirke Aboth and what else of the same kind there is in the Mishna connects itself in form and subject-matter with Proverbs and Ecclesiastes. But while this sacred book of later Judaism was thus content to rest almost entirely on only a part of the Old Testament, the Gospels virtually connect themselves with the whole; with the Pentateuch, notably in the Sermon on the Mount, with the Prophets, especially in St Matthew, who definitely writes on the principle that Christ and His teaching are the fulfilling of the prophets; with Psalms in frequent quotations; with Proverbs in those sayings of 'worldly wisdom' that are not rare in Christ's teaching. The relation of the Gospels to the historical books of the Old Testament is brought out most clearly in the speeches in the Acts, where the history of the Old Testament is appealed to as leading up to the Gospel.

Moreover while the Mishna elaborates the Law with a servile regard for the letter, tempered by an ingenious casuistry, the Gospel uses the spirit of the Old Testament as the means of advancing in the freedom of the Spirit to new developments of higher teaching.

The difference as to the amount of the Old Testament dealt with is carried out in quotations. While the Gospel quotes nearly the whole range of the books of the Old Testament with certainly no preference for the Pentateuch, the Mishna rarely refers to anything else but the Pentateuch. But the Canon of the Mishna and of the Gospels are essentially the same, and identical with that of our Bible.

In both Mishna and Gospel the authority of the Old Testament is rather taken for granted than definitely stated, and both assume on the part of the hearer or reader a considerable knowledge of scripture. The Mishna never states the text it is discussing and assumes that the reader will be so familiar with it as to know from the discussion itself what point is under consideration. *Authority of the Old Testament.*

With the above limitations we may say that the Mishna, like the Gospels, has many ordinary straightforward quotations, in which the Old Testament is appealed to as an authority, or used to illustrate some point of doctrine or ceremony. *Quotations, Method, &c.*

But even in the New Testament there are quotations where sentences are used without reference to their meaning and context in the Old Testament because the words describe or illustrate the New Testament. As for instance when the words 'Out of Egypt have I called my son' are applied to the return of the infant Christ from Egypt, though in the original it applies to the children of Israel, and is part of a reproach against their ingratitude. We shall see further on that the Mishna is more systematically and dogmatically indifferent to the context of its quotations so long as a meaning can be extracted from the words.

Again, in the Gospels we find words and phrases of the Old Testament constantly embedded in the language. Naturally in the Mishna the influence of the Old Testament on the language shows itself chiefly in the use of the terms and phrases of the Law.

Forced application.

We find however in the Mishna much use of scripture of a very artificial kind. Every word, every letter is considered pregnant with meaning, the arrangement of the words, the use of the singular for the plural, everything is full of meaning. On the one hand we read in the Gemara 'There are no two passages in the Law which repeat the same thing'[1], and on the other, it is desirable to prove everything from the Law. Hence the different forms of synonymous expressions are pressed to give essentially different meanings, and the most casual expressions in a simple narrative are treated as the deliberate and permanently binding enunciations of important truths. If this fails poetry is interpreted by mystical or allegorical formulæ. For instance 'I will bring your sanctuaries into desolation'; the fact that in this sentence the sanctuaries are spoken of and it is not expressly stated that they cease to be sanctuaries is held to prove that they remain sanctuaries even when desolate[2].

[1] Sanhedrin Gemara, fol. 39, Klein.
[2] Megillah III. 3.

Then again it is desired to find scriptural authority for the way of saying the Shema and it is found thus: 'Beth Shammai hold, that in the evening, men are to recline when they say the Shema, and in the morning they are to stand upright; for it is said, When thou liest down and when thou risest up. But Beth Hillel hold that every man is to say it in his own way, in what posture he pleases, for it is said When thou walkest by the way. Such being the case why then is it said, When thou liest down and when thou risest up. The meaning is at the time when mankind usually lie down and at the time when they usually rise up[1]".

Reason for a liturgical practice is found as follows: "The exit from Egypt is to be mentioned at night. Rabbi Eleazar ben Azariah saith, Verily I am almost seventy years of age, but have not succeeded in proving that the exit from Egypt ought to be mentioned at night until Ben Zoma expounded, That thou mayest remember the day of thy going forth from the land of Egypt all the days of thy life. 'The days of thy life' would denote the days only; but the expression 'all the days of thy life' includes the night likewise. But the Sages say 'the days of thy life' denote the present state; whereas 'all the days of thy life' include the future days of the Messiah[2]". Compare also the following, 'Whence know we that Achan's confession made atonement for him? As it is said, And Joshua said Why hast thou troubled us? The Lord shall trouble thee this day. This day art thou troubled but thou shalt not be troubled in the world to come[3]'.

These are only one or two examples out of a large number.

---

[1] Berachoth I. 3.   [2] Berachoth I. 5.
[3] Sanhedrin VI. 2.

106 RELATION OF THE MISHNA TO THE OLD TESTAMENT.

Alterations. The Mishna in one or two instances uses a text to suggest a new truth by altering some prominent word. 'And it saith And the tables were the work of God, and the writing was the writing of God, graven upon the tables. Read not Charuth graven but Cheruth freedom, for thou wilt find no freeman but him who is occupied in learning Torah[1]'.

Rationalism. In the explanations already quoted of the Fiery Serpent and of Moses' prayer at Rephidim we see traces of a rationalising spirit.

Additions. It is interesting to notice in what different ways the Gospels and the Mishna supplement the Old Testament. The Gospels add nothing to the history, little or nothing to ritual or legal observance, elaborates none of these, but develops great principles, supplies additional motives and inspires new hopes. The Mishna fills up and completes with great elaboration the scheme of law, and even extends its list of miracles into Old Testament times and tells of the wonderful things which were created at the moment of transition from the six days of creation to the first Sabbath.

[1] Pirke Aboth VI. 2.

CHAPTER X.

SUBSEQUENT HISTORY OF THE MISHNA AND THE GOSPELS.

IN tracing the subsequent history of the Mishna and the Gospels, and noting such points in the history of each as offer ground for comparison, we must remember that they originated approximately in similar circumstances and the same period of time. Both are in a measure due to the inspiration of the Messianic age, but in very different ways. The Gospels breath an atmosphere of success and are full of undiminished hope. The Mishna as we have it succeeds to the failure of attempts to realize the Messianic kingdom; the hope within it is but faint and it has more of the stern resolution that may be gathered from despair. Yet the glories of Christianity ought not to make us altogether blind to the invincible patriotism, the heroic pertinacity with which the teachers of this ruined and scattered people renewed the grasp of the Law upon the conscience of Israel and secured the unity and persistence of Jewish life and worship. *Circumstances of origin.*

The first prominent feature in the history of the Mishna is the formation of a mass of literature relating to it. This literature eventually was arranged as a kind of commentary to the Mishna and appeared in two recensions known as the *Gemara.*

Jerusalem and Babylonian Talmud respectively. As the new matter was similar in character, equal in merit and often superior in interest to the Mishna itself, it came to have an almost equal authority, and the sacred book was not the Mishna merely, but the Mishna and its commentary, i.e. the Talmud. Henceforward the history of the Mishna is for the most part the history of the Talmud. This new development, together with the original Mishna, extends to six or eight large folio volumes, and the style is at least as obscure as that of the Mishna; so that it became simply impossible that it should be used as a popular text-book, and its authority served chiefly to increase the influence of the limited class who had leisure and learning enough to study it. Now in the case of the Gospels it is true that the Acts, Epistles and Apocalypse were added to them and they became one book, but these are in no way parallel to the Gemara. Another mass of Christian literature arose dealing with the New Testament, namely the Patristic writings, and these formed a sort of Christian Gemara. In time a supplementary authority was accorded to the Fathers as interpreters of the New Testament; but their writings were different in character, far inferior both in merit and interest to the Gospels; their bulk became even more formidable than that of the Talmud. Hence the New Testament has never had the dead weight of the Patristic writings tied round its neck in the shape of a commentary of coordinate authority published with it; and the Churches of the Reformation have strictly limited the authority to be accorded to the Fathers. Nevertheless when we speak disparagingly of the Talmud, its many volumes, its tedious frivolity of allegorical interpretation and petty detail, its doubtful casuistry, we should remember that the Fathers are not altogether free from similar faults. Allegorical interpretation of the wildest character is to be found in the Epistle of Barnabas and the writings of Ambrose; the casuistry of Chrysostom is more than doubtful at times, and Jerome distinguishes himself by bitter and unscrupulous partisanship. From these a Jewish writer might compile a selection of passages as absurd as some of those popular sets of extracts from the Talmud, which, to the mind of a Jew, might seem intended to pander to Christian prejudices or to supply the perennial craving of the human mind for trivial anecdotes. But however tainted with such faults both Talmud and Fathers helped to throw new light on ancient truth, and it is only the false use which may be made of them which makes them stumbling blocks to Jew and Christian respectively.

The Mishna being now absorbed in the Talmud, the latter became the representative book of the Jews, as the New Testament was of the Christians, and as both Jews and Christians were emphatically what has been called religions of a book, it was natural that the enemy of the religion should seek to destroy the book. It is well known that the last great persecution of the Christians, that of Diocletian, specially aimed at the destruction of the New Testament, and in the days of the Reformation and since a similar object has been attempted by those who believed that a New Testament in the vernacular was a dangerous and fatal book to place in the hands of the laity. In like manner the enemies of Judaism have again and again struck at the Talmud. Justinian forbad the use of the Mishna[1]. Under Pope Julius III. the Talmud was ordered to be burned[2]. At the *Destruction of sacred books.*

[1] Milman, *Hist. of Jews*, III. 75.   [2] III. 343.

revival of learning at the Reformation, when printed editions began to be issued and Reuchlin devoted himself to the study of Rabbinical writings, a great outcry was raised both against the writings and against the faithless Christian who so far forgot himself as to study them. But fortunately Reuchlin, aided by the influence of Erasmus, and protected by the Archbishop of Maintz, was able more or less to hold his own. Luther's advice was to take away all their Talmuds in which are nothing but godlessness, lies, cursing and swearing[1].

By order of the Council of Trent subsequent editions of the Talmud were purged of attacks on the Christians. It is very much the fashion to speak of the absence of these attacks from later editions as due to the anxiety of modern Jews to suppress the evidence of former intolerance. This motive may have its weight now, but it is only fair to remember to whom the original expurgation was due.

It cannot be doubted that, as the persecution of Diocletian helped to establish the authority of the New Testament, so these efforts, on the part of the enemies of Judaism, to destroy the Talmud only emphasized its authority and secured for it the devoted attachment of the Jews.

Karaites. But while these attacks were made from outside there were not wanting Jews who protested against the authority of this superadded mass of tradition. As in the history of the Church we meet with occasional protests against the authority of the Fathers, and later on against that of the schoolmen, so from the eighth century the existence of the Karaites[2] was a standing protest against the authority alike of Mishna and Gemara. This sect of the Jews fell back on

[1] Milman, *Hist. Jews*, III. 353.   [2] III. 126.

THE MISHNA AND THE GOSPELS.

the Old Testament as the Reformers on the New Testament, but their influence was as limited though more continuous than that of the pre-Reformation Protestants.

In spite of opposition both the Gospels and the Talmud fulfilled their missions. As a product of a living hope and a means of its fulfilment, the Gospels continually extended the sphere of their influence; the hope had been an aggressive one, and claimed that its influence should be world-wide. The book succeeded in its mission. But the object of the Mishna and subsequently of the Talmud was entirely different. It was not intended to gather in converts to Judaism, it was rather a means by which the Jewish people retired still more within itself and drew around itself ever tightening bonds, which while they secured the union of the people, also shut out the Gentiles from them. It has been for centuries entirely successful; absorbed in what seem to the Christian the unattractive and multitudinous formulæ of his life and worship, the Jew has been continually reminded of his unique position and special calling; he has remained separate and preserved a national character. *[How the Gospels and the Talmud fulfilled their respective missions.]*

Nor has the influence of the Talmud been confined to the Jews. The Talmud exercised considerable influence on and supplied materials for the Koran. The teaching which was afterwards embodied in the Talmud even acted upon Christianity itself through the medium of some of the Gnostic sects. The Cabbalistic portions of the Talmud and other Rabbinical writings had their share in the popular magic of the Middle Ages. In our own days the Talmud is a storehouse of quaint suggestions for poets and is used for the illustration and interpretation of both Old and New Testament. *[Influence on the Koran and on Christian literature.]*

Hebrew the language of worship and of the Sacred Books.

The influence of the Talmud was and to a very large extent is even yet limited by the absence of translations. As in the Church of the Middle Ages so among the Jews the sacred books and the liturgies were hidden from the laity under the veil of an unknown language. It is true that Hebrew has always been known amongst the Jews to a much larger extent than Latin amongst the Christians, still there would doubtless be a proportion in old times as there is a large proportion now, who could only understand a Hebrew liturgy through a translation. Moreover the language of the Talmud needs special study even in those who are familiar with Biblical Hebrew. Thus just as the Latin liturgies and the Vulgate were the mysterious and magical weapons of a priestly caste and served to invest their person and authority with a supernatural awe, so in a smaller degree the Hebrew liturgies and the Talmud exalted the Rabbis.

Commentaries.

But the Talmud needs not only translations but commentaries. What commentaries exist are chiefly on the Mishna, they are comparatively few and aim rather at explaining the text, than at preaching sermons on it. It is needless to say that the older commentaries are in Rabbinical Hebrew. As the Mediaeval Church looked on the knowledge of the New Testament as an esoteric book to be reserved for the study of the profound scholar or the privileged ecclesiastic, so the study of the Mishna was not intended for any but those sufficiently imbued with the spirit of Judaism to be familiar with the Jewish language.

Influence of the Renascence, Translations,

The general revival of learning at the Renascence extended its influence to Judaism. Christians took up the study of Jewish literature and gradually the Talmud was

THE MISHNA AND THE GOSPELS.   113

made somewhat more accessible to the student. Buxtorf published his great lexicon. And as the Renascence gave rise to English and German translations of the Bible, so, only considerably later, Surenhusius in the 17th century translated[1] the Mishna and some of its commentaries (not the Gemara) into Latin, and somewhat earlier a Spanish version was published. In the seventeenth century the Mishna was translated into German, and in 1845 eighteen treatises were translated into English by Rabbis de Sola and Raphall, and other portions have been translated. The Talmud is now being translated into French by Moise Schwabe.

<small>Commentaries, and Lexicons.</small>

How far the influence of the Talmud will survive the loss of the safe shelter of an unknown language, how far it could subsist by its own merits, if the belief on external grounds in its divine authority were lost, a Christian is scarcely in a position to judge. The New Testament can be read by everybody in almost every language and still maintains its influence even over those who deny its special claims to divine authority.

<small>Effect of translation.</small>

Doubtless modern criticism makes the New Testament more and more dependent on the inherent vitality of its teaching as witnessed to and enforced by the Divine Spirit in the human spirit, and similar causes are breaking down the authority of traditional Judaism and of the Talmud amongst the Jews. But the failure of the faith of the Jews in Judaism is not due to any extension of the influence of Christianity but to the working of those forces which attack alike all revelations. Moreover it should be remembered

<small>Modern Rationalism and Criticism.</small>

---

[1] It is said that the Talmud was translated into Arabic in the 10th century, but the use of this would be limited. Milman, *Hist. Jews*, III. 147.

B.   8

114 SUBSEQUENT HISTORY OF THE MISHNA AND GOSPELS.

The Future.

that the surrender of one faith is seldom the immediate introduction to another. There seems good reason to suppose that side by side in the future as in the past Christianity and Judaism will bear their mutual witness to each other and their common witness to the eternal working of the Divine Spirit.

APPENDIX.

I. THE SECOND COMING OF THE SON OF MAN AND THE ADVENT OF THE JEWISH MESSIAH.

A comparison may be made between the signs of the coming of the Son of Man as given by Christ and those of the coming of the Messiah as given by the Mishna. The signs of the coming of the Son of Man are these: 'There shall be great distress upon the land, and wrath unto this people. And they shall fall by the edge of the sword, and shall be led captive unto all the nations; and Jerusalem shall be trodden down of the Gentiles, until the times of the Gentiles be fulfilled. And there shall be signs in sun and moon and stars; and upon the earth distress of nations, in perplexity for the roaring of the sea and the billows; men fainting for fear, and for expectation of the things which are coming on the world: for the powers of the heavens shall be shaken. And then shall they see the Son of Man coming in a cloud with power and great glory[1]'.

In the Mishna we read: 'Shortly before the advent of the Messiah licence shall increase; prices shall be very high; the vine

[1] S. Luke xxi. 23—27.

shall bring forth fruit, yet wine shall be dear. And the kingdom shall be overthrown by heresy and there shall be no reproof.. ... and the territory of Judæa shall be desolate and its borders shall be laid waste. Distinguished men shall go about from city to city and shall meet with no kindness, the wisdom of the doctors of the law shall grow rotten, they that fear sin shall be despised and there shall be great lack of truth, youths shall put to shame old men, old men shall rise up before youths. The son shall provoke the father, the daughter shall rise up against her mother, and the daughter-in-law against her mother-in-law, and a man's foes shall be they of his own household[1]. That generation shall be shameless as a dog, nor shall the son respect his father. Whom then shall we trust? Our Father who is in heaven[2]'.

II. ILLUSTRATIVE QUOTATIONS.

S. Matthew vi. 3, 'When thou doest alms, let not thy left hand know what thy right hand doeth'.

Shekalim v. 6, 'There was a chamber for secret almsgiving wherein pious men put gifts for the nourishing of the deserving poor'.

S. Matthew vi. 26, 'Behold the birds of the heaven, that they sow not, neither do they reap, nor gather into barns; and your heavenly Father feedeth them. Are not ye of much more value than they'?

Kedushin iv. 14, "Rabbi Simeon ben Eleazar said, 'Didst thou ever see any animal or bird exercise any trade or handicraft and yet they are maintained without trouble or care; they were created to serve me; would it not follow, that I, who was created for the sole purpose of worshipping my Creator, should also find my maintenance without trouble, if it were not that, through my evil conduct, I have forfeited my maintenance'".

---

[1] Micah vii. 6, 7; Matt. x. 35, 36.   [2] Sotah ix. 15.

S. Matthew vii. 2, 'With what measure ye mete it shall be measured unto you'.

Sotah i. 7, 'With what measure a man measureth, with that do they measure unto him'.

S. Matthew ix. 17, 'Neither do men put new wine into old wine-skins: else the skins burst, and the wine is spilled, and the skins perish: but they put new wine into fresh wine-skins, and both are preserved'.

Yadaim iv. 3, 'Let therefore one new regulation be subjected to conclusions drawn from another new regulation; but let not a new regulation be subjected to conclusions drawn from an old established regulation'.

S. Mark v. 25, 26, 'A woman, which had an issue of blood twelve years, and had suffered many things of many physicians, and had spent all that she had, and was nothing bettered but rather grew worse'.

Kedushin iv. 14, 'R. Judah says in the name of Abba Guriah ......the best of physicians is destined for Gehinnom'.

RR. de Sola and Raphall are careful to note that this has not the force of a law, but is merely an expression of private opinion.

S. Luke i. 21, 'And the people were waiting for Zacharias, and they marvelled while he tarried in the temple'.

Yoma v. 1, 'He (the High Priest on the Day of Atonement) ......offered a shorter prayer in the outer house, and he did not prolong his prayer, lest he should excite terror in Israel'.

'Terror', that is to say, lest some divine judgment had befallen him.

www.ingramcontent.com/pod-product-compliance
Lightning Source LLC
Chambersburg PA
CBHW020122170426
43199CB00009B/604